ENGLISH
COMIC DRAMA
1700–1750

ENGLISH
COMIC DRAMA
1700–1750

BY

F. W. BATESON

New York

RUSSELL & RUSSELL

1963

FIRST PUBLISHED IN 1929
REISSUED, 1963, BY RUSSELL & RUSSELL, INC.
BY ARRANGEMENT WITH THE AUTHOR
L.C. CATALOG CARD NO: 63-8357

PRINTED IN THE UNITED STATES OF AMERICA

FOR EMILY WILLIAMSON

CONTENTS

I

INTRODUCTION

i

A CURIOUS ceremony ushered in the eighteenth century in England. By the old calendar the new century began on the 25th of March 1700, and on the evening of the 25th an inaugural pageant, in the form of a kind of allegorical ballet, was produced at Drury Lane, printed copies being 'deliver'd Gratis at the Theatre'. The moving spirits in the affair seem to have been Dryden and Vanbrugh, and probably Colley Cibber. The text was published again in June with the title, 'A Secular Masque', and the information that it had been 'Written by the late Great Poet Mr. Dryden, just before his Death, being the last of his Works'. The masque, in itself and because of the circumstances of its origin, is one of the most remarkable 'documents' in the history of criticism. Its interest is its self-consciousness. It might plausibly be described as a *post mortem* by the age upon itself. It is a deliberate and considered epitome of the civilization of the preceding hundred years; and it exhibits for the last time that quality, or combination of qualities, which had distinguished their literature. From one point of view, indeed, the poem may be taken as a *pièce de justification*. The declamation by Diana beginning,

With Horns and with Hounds I waken the Day,
And hye to my Woodland walks away :
I tuck up my Robe, and am buskined soon,
And tye to my Forehead a wexing Moon,

and the more familiar lines to Mars,

> Thy Sword within the Scabbard keep,
> And let Mankind agree;
> Better the World were fast asleep,
> Than kept awake by Thee,

are especially significant. They have, to the full, the vigour and the concision which are the rule in Dryden's verse ; and they have the lyrical note, an Elizabethan aftertaste, which is the exception. It is at once a compendium of the achievements of the past and a challenge to the future. From another point of view the poem is a confession of failure. Its interest from this aspect is that it is a declaration of the bankruptcy of the Restoration ideals by the poet who had most successfully embodied them. A framework is provided, in the manner of the time, by a number of mythological figures—Diana, Mars, Venus, Momus, Janus, Chronos; but except as a framework the *dramatis personae* are irrelevant. The real subject of the 'Secular Masque' is the retrospective criticism which is implied in the title. The earlier years of the century—

> A very Merry, Dancing, Drinking,
> Laughing, Quaffing, and unthinking Time,

are represented by Diana. A shabby and disillusioned Mars presides over the Civil Wars—

> The Fools are only thinner,
> With all our Cost and Care;
> But neither side a winner,
> For Things are as they were.

And the Restoration and after, when 'Joy rul'd the Day, and Love the Night', is under the aegis of

Venus. It is, however, Momus, who may be assumed
to represent Dryden himself, who pronounces the
verdict:—

	All, all, of a piece throughout;
Pointing to *Diana*.	Thy Chase had a Beast in View ;
to *Mars*.	Thy Wars brought nothing about ;
to *Venus*.	Thy Lovers were all untrue.

And Janus and Chronos chime in:—

> 'Tis well an Old Age is out.
> And time to begin a New.

It is evident that Dryden recognized that a revolution was in the air (in thought even more than in
politics), which he welcomed, although he could not
formulate it. The outlines are clearer to-day. In
political terms the seventeenth century had been an
epoch of expansion. The 'New' age, which Dryden
prophesied but did not live to share, was to be an
epoch of concentration, and the new literature was
the suave and ordered literature which is the inevitable, if not always the essential, expression of such
a period. It was Augustan, with all that word implies
of polish and grace, mannerisms and superficialities.
In one direction, indeed, the new century represented
only a weakening of the old qualities, a watering down
almost. It was sophisticated, where the Restoration
had been sceptical, an age of gallantry following upon
one of sensuality ; it was rationalistic, where the
Restoration had been intellectual, hypocritical where
that had been brutal. The ideal ceased to be the
' wit ', ' a Compound ', in Farquhar's words, ' of
practical Rake and speculative Gentleman '; it became, in a reflection of the *honnête homme* of the
French, the ' man of sense '. A contempt for insin-

cerity was common to both centuries; but the contempt which had been confined to the insincerity which consists in a distrust of the senses, to the

> Reason, an *Ignis fatuus* of the Mind,
> Which leaves the Light of Nature, Sense, behind,

was transferred, with a loss of logic, to the 'enthusiasm' in which a half-hearted rationalism found its antithesis. In literature the change consisted primarily in a diminution of intensity; it is the difference between Rochester's

> Dear; from thine Arms then let me flie,
> That my fantastick Mind may prove,
> The Torments it deserves to try,
> That tears my fixt Heart from my Love,

and Prior's

> What Nymph shou'd I admire, or trust,
> But Cloe Beauteous, Cloe Just?
> What Nymph should I desire to see,
> But Her who leaves the Plain for Me?
> To Whom shou'd I compose the Lay,
> But Her who listens, when I play?

As verse there is much to be said for Prior's lines; as poetry they are immeasurably inferior. But the difference is one, not of kind, but of degree; Rochester's 'fantastick Mind', reduced in the poetic scale, is not far from the whimsicality of Prior. A revolution of taste lies between the two poems; but it is a comparatively domestic revolution; it has left the essentials where they were.

The eighteenth century was, in this sense, an emasculated reproduction of the Restoration; but it was something more. The rococo prettifications, which have been popularized by the de Goncourts in

France and by Austin Dobson in England, are at the best a half-truth. A profound seriousness was not less typical of the age. There was Young as well as Prior, Wesley as well as Horace Walpole. It is true the period was not serious in the nineteenth-century sense ; that is to say, it was not solemn. A seriousness which reposes as securely upon its convictions can dispense with solemnity. The importance of the eighteenth century from this aspect is its discovery, or rediscovery, of what can only be called the social sense. The seventeenth century, as a whole, had been vigorously and aggressively individualistic. The society which is mirrored in Restoration literature, and particularly in the Restoration comedies, is still in a state of nature; love is a battle of the sexes. The individual, with his oddities and eccentricities, is emphasized ; the *milieu* is overlooked. Satire, instead of being a criticism of the individual upon his failure to conform to a social norm, tends to become the expression of a personal hostility ; essentially, it is invective. With the eighteenth century the emphasis changes altogether. A detail, which is significantly typical, is the contrast of the points of view of two opponents of the duel in the two periods. For the Restoration there is Rochester's epigram,

> Meerly for Safety, after Fame they thirst ;
> For all Men would be Cowards if they durst ;

for the eighteenth century there is Steele's objection in *The Tatler* to 'a Custom which all Men wish exploded, tho' no Man has Courage enough to resist it '. The reasoning is the same in both cases, but the underlying motives are exactly opposite ; Rochester's is the protest of the individual, Steele's is that of

society. There is the same antithesis in the pessi-
mistic philosophies that are to some extent characteristic of both the 'New' and the 'Old Age'. The
pessimism of the eighteenth century found its most
trenchant expression in Swift's 'I cannot but conclude
the Bulk of your Natives to be the most pernicious
Race of little odious Vermin that Nature ever suffered
to crawl upon the Surface of the Earth'. It is not
always remembered that the vices which elicited the
verdict of the King of Brobdingnag were Parliamen-
tarianism, militarism, sectarianism, high finance—in a
word, the social vices. The pessimism of the Restoration was more profound :—

> Were I, who to my cost, already am,
> One of those strange, prodigious Creatures Man;
> A Spirit free, to choose for my own share,
> What sort of Flesh and Blood I pleas'd to wear,
> I'd be a Dog, a Monkey or a Bear.

The enemy, then, was not man the 'political animal',
but the human reason itself.

In the eighteenth century it was the group, of
which the individual was only a unit, which came
first, and as a consequence a new quality was developed. It may be called a heightened social con-
sciousness, a sensitiveness at once to the claims of
one's neighbours, and to an abstract ideal of order.
In politics the change was reflected in an increase of
the national self-consciousness; John Bull was an
eighteenth-century invention. In the drama it con-
jured into being the disturbing spirit which we now
call 'sentimentalism'.

ii

Charles Lamb's essay 'On the Artificial Comedy of the last Century' has been disparaged by the critics because of a certain exaggeration of emphasis. It is still, however, the most acute analysis we have of the *idea*, the quiddity, of Restoration comedy. It is the essence, Lamb saw, of the comedies of Congreve and his companions, not that they are indecent, not that they are cynical, but that they are deliberately passionless and artificial, 'a speculative scene of things, which has no reference whatever to the world that is'. Foppington and Horner, Dorimant and Foresight, are not the habitants of this earth, but of an aerial, fantastic fairyland. We cannot identify ourselves in their escapades, and we have no ambition to emulate their extravagances. It is true that we are willing to accept them for the moment, but it is as hypotheses, not as actualities; as figures of the fancy, not less mythical and not less remote than the centaur or the sphinx.

The revolution which 'sentimentalism' effected was precisely to exile from the theatre this happy-go-lucky, butterfly existence. It brought back a sense of responsibility into the dramatic world. It invited the spectator to come up again on to the stage, and to recognize in the *dramatis personae* his brothers and sisters—people confronted with the same problems as himself, paralysed by the same weaknesses, redeemed by the same generosities. 'Sentimentalism' meant the return of what we may call sympathy to the theatre; it restored to comedy the humanity which the Restoration had suppressed. The earlier dramatists had created characters in whom their audience could only half believe in situations in which it was impossible to believe at all. With Hoyden and Sir Tunbelly in their country house, with Lady Wishfort at her *toilette*, with Horner and his china, there is no question of probability at all. It is irrelevant and disturbing, and the defiance of the probabilities is one of the principal sources of the piquancy of these episodes. In the sentimental comedies of Cibber and Steele the question of probability is everything. It is essential to their success that we can believe in and identify ourselves with the characters they have created. We must be able to put ourselves in the place of Sir Charles Easy when he discovers his wife's steinkirk on his head. We must be induced to sympathize with Bevil's refusal to fight his duel with Myrtle.

'Sentimentalism' has been defined by Mr. Allardyce Nicoll as ' the presentation of a moral problem ', and again as ' the relating of art to life ; the return to a highly artificial love of natural scenery and rural landscape ; and the deliberate enunciation of a moral or social problem '. Mr. Bernbaum, on the other hand, in his extremely valuable investigation, *The Drama of Sensibility*, has limited ' the mainspring of sentimentalism ' to a ' confidence in the goodness of average human nature '. There is nothing to object to in either of these definitions, except perhaps Mr. Nicoll's introduction of ' natural scenery and rural landscape ', which are among the symptoms rather than the sources of the sentimental point of view. But the implications of the definitions are wider than their authors seem to have realized. The rise of ' sentimentalism ' coincided with the attacks of Jeremy Collier and his fellow moralists on the immorality and profaneness of the stage. Undoubtedly the sentimental dramatists sympathized with these attacks. Cibber applauds Collier in his *Apology*, and Steele, in assailing Etherege in *The Spectator*, was only carrying Collier's programme to its logical conclusion. It is easy to understand the source of this sympathy. The sentimental dramatists, by once again making comedy a mirror of life, had necessarily brought into it the moral laws which govern life. But the movements, none the less, were distinct and not the same. There is no reason to believe that Collier ever approved of any of the sentimental comedies; it is certain that he disapproved of the highly sentimental *Love's Last Shift* of Cibber. It will be remembered that Macaulay, the advocate of Collier, was of the opinion that the indecency of Restoration comedy, 'though perpetually such as is condemned not less by the rules of good taste than by those of morality, is not, in our opinion, so disgraceful a fault as its singularly inhuman spirit'. In drawing this distinction, however, Macaulay was unconsciously parting company with Collier. As a moralist Collier was indifferent to the inhumanity of the Restoration dramatists; it was their indecency to which he objected. But if the distinction would have seemed irrelevant to him, it would have been welcomed by the sentimental dramatists. The truth is that Cibber and Steele, like Macaulay himself, were humanitarians first of all. The decency or indecency of their plays was a secondary consideration. And as a matter of fact, as was pointed out by the acute Dennis, 'sentimentalism' had its own immorality. 'Obscenity', Dennis remarked, 'cannot be very dangerous, because it is rude and shocking;

but Love is a Passion; which is so agreeable to the movements of corrupted Nature, that by seeing it livelily touched and often represented, an Amorous disposition insensibly insinuates itself into the chastest Breast'. Cibber and Steele were not infrequently guilty of this immorality. Steele, indeed, under the disguise of a 'Constant Reader', condemned his own Campley for precisely this reason. 'I was last Night', he wrote in *The Spectator*, 'at the *Funeral*, where a Confident Lover in the Play, speaking of his Mistress, cries out—Oh that Harriot! to fold these Arms about the Waste of that Beauteous strugling, and at last yielding Fair! Such an Image as this ought, by no means, to be presented to a Chaste and Regular Audience.' In later editions of *The Funeral* the passage was cut down to, 'Oh that Harriot! to embrace that Beauteous—'. The celebrated steinkirk scene in *The Careless Husband*, one of the pinnacles of sentimental comedy, suffered in much the same way for much the same reason. 'There is something too gross', observed the amiable Derrick, echoing apparently the opinions prevailing in the middle of the century, 'in shewing Sir Charles Easy and Edging asleep in a bed-chamber; and though it furnishes an incident that illustrates the character of Lady Easy, decency would forgive the exhibition'. At Dublin the feeling went so far that Lady Easy was introduced 'as if seeing this scene at a distance, so that they are not brought forward; but Sir Charles enters with the handkerchief in his hand, and the reflections that are put into his mouth very naturally follow: the confusion of Edging is sufficiently shewn in her running across the Stage when the bell rings'. The fact is that the primary object of 'sentimentalism' was to humanize the drama, whereas the primary object of Collier was to make it didactic. Unfortunately, neither Steele nor Cibber nor any of their followers defined to themselves what they were doing. In England a revolution, whether it is in literature or in politics, is rarely self-conscious. In consequence one sometimes gets the impression that the sentimental dramatists looked upon themselves as the disciples of Collier. The connexion was not really fundamental, but accidental. They were allies, but the methods they employed and the ends they proposed were never identical.

iii

There is a reservation which requires to be made. 'Sentimentalism' is the quality which *differentiates* the dramatists of the eighteenth century from those of the Restoration; as a formula to *explain* them it is inadequate. The fact is that their loyalties were still divided. The sentimental elements which are to be found in their plays did not involve a more than partial or momentary espousal of the sentimental *idea*. Mr. Galsworthy and Sir James Barrie in our own times have approached nearer to that *idea* than Cibber or even Steele. Indeed, Cibber's *The Refusal* is an amusing caricature of sentimental excesses. The tone of the age was not predominantly sentimental. The enthusiasm with which *Love's Last Shift* and *The Conscious Lovers* were welcomed has obscured the undercurrent of criticism which was not less typical and which was certainly not less general. The reaction had begun as early as 1702 with the objections of *A Comparison between the Two Stages* to the 'too affecting' images in *The Funeral*. It is

explicit in the critical essays of Dennis, and in particular in the *Remarks on a Play, call'd, The Conscious
Lovers*. It extends to Goldsmith's ironical recipe for
a successful comedy. 'It is only sufficient', he
observed, 'to raise the Characters a little, to deck
out the Hero with a Ribbon, or give the Heroine
a Title; then to put an Insipid Dialogue, without
Character or Humour, into their mouths, give them
mighty good hearts, very fine clothes, furnish a new
set of Scenes, make a Pathetic Scene or two, with
a sprinkling of tender Melancholy Conversation
through the whole, and there is no doubt but all
the Ladies will cry, and all the Gentlemen applaud.'
The genuine comedy of sentiment was the *comédie
larmoyante* of Nivelle de la Chaussée, which was not
naturalized in England until the later years of the
century. The dramatists of Anne and the first
Georges were still faithful, in their various ways and
in different degrees, to the traditions of comedy
which had been established at the Restoration. The
'manners' comedy of Etherege and Congreve, the
'intrigue' comedy which is associated with Aphra
Behn, the burlesque of the type set by *The Rehearsal*,
persisted, though with diminished vitality. The
drama was divided against itself. The fact explains
the lack of consistency, the failure to achieve a unity
of tone and impression, which is the most serious
defect in the comedies of the eighteenth century.
It was not, indeed, in the theatre, but in the essays
of Steele and Shaftesbury and the novels of Richardson and Sterne, that 'sentimentalism' received its
fullest and perfected expression.

The centre of gravity was not 'sentimentalism'
but the humanitarianism, the heightened social con-

sciousness which had made 'sentimentalism' possible. 'Sentimentalism' was an exaggeration, or a distortion, of the profounder and more general movement which was humanizing the life and literature of the time. The institution of Sunday schools and the beginnings of prison reform are one aspect of this movement. The essays of Addison and the novels of Defoe and Fielding are another aspect of the same movement, and Sir Roger de Coverley, Robinson Crusoe, and Parson Adams are its typical creations. They are not precisely characters of sentiment, like Lady Easy and Bevil; but they derive from the same origin. They fulfil a similar purpose; they point, with infinitely more success, the same moral. (The flesh and blood of palpable and plausible human beings necessarily proved better arguments for 'the goodness of average human nature' than the diffident abstractions which were deliberately created for the purpose.) There is the same distinction in the comedies themselves. By the side of the repentant scapegraces and the drooping heroines there are figures like Farquhar's Kite and Cherry, Steele's Humphry Gubbin and Biddy Tipkin, Gay's Polly and Macheath. The dramatists had begun to laugh with, instead of at, their *dramatis personae*. The callousness and cynicism of the Restoration, tending always to satirical caricature, had disappeared, and a certain freshness and humour had taken their place. It is this humour and this freshness which are at the heart of eighteenth-century comedy. Against the charges of didacticism and sentimentality they provide its justification. In so far, that is to say, as the didactic and sentimental elements become important in a play, it will tend to be an aberration from the comic norm.

II

COLLEY CIBBER

i

IT is recorded that 'Pope was heard to say in his last sickness—"My satires against Cibber, are not my last repented faults"'. The anecdote is perhaps apocryphal. It is certain, at any rate, that his penitence, whether genuine or assumed, has been as unavailing as Cibber's own *Apology* and the rehabilitations of Hazlitt and Isaac Disraeli to dignify Colley Cibber in the eyes of posterity. The name still conjures up the odious and fantastic figure that Pope crowned, in succession to Theobald, the prince of his dunces:—

> What then remains? Ourself. Still, still remain
> Cibberian forehead, and Cibberian brain.
> This brazen Brightness, to the 'Squire so dear;
> This polish'd Hardness, that reflects the Peer:
> This arch Absurd, that wit and fool delights;
> This Mess, toss'd up of Hockley-hole and White's.

The caricature has impressed itself impregnably in the popular imagination; it seems to be impossible to lay its ghost. The Cibber we know is still the fop,

> form'd by nature, Stage and Town to bless,
> And act, and be, a Coxcomb with success,

the remorseless plagiarist of 'poor Fletcher's half-eat scenes' and the 'Frippery of crucify'd Moliere', and the 'never-blushing', self-appointed 'Lord Chancellor of Plays'. The fact is a tribute to Pope's art; he has defied history and verisimilitude with complete success. And yet the portrait is not among the masterpieces in his satirical gallery. It is confused; it lacks the consistency and the minute plausibility of his Atticus and his Sporus; the outlines are blurred. I am not even certain how serious Pope was. The conception of a 'lively Dunce', a combination of the dullard and the impertinent, was a contradiction in terms the effectiveness of which must have depended upon its paradoxicality. Instead of the conviction which is induced in genuine satire, it can only have stimulated surprise.

The origin of Pope's hostility is still disputed. Perhaps, as Hazlitt has suggested, it was a matter of temperament, an instinctive revulsion before high spirits and a thick skin. To some extent, however, it must certainly have been a quite impersonal reflection of the extraordinary unpopularity which enveloped Cibber. It is remarkable how very few people seem to have liked him. The kindly Steele once observed with regret 'a strong Inclination and Propensity of the Town to receive with Pleasure any thing that tends to the Personal Mortification of Mr. Cibber', and there is plenty of evidence that he was not exaggerating. An epilogue which was written for the younger Killigrew's *Chit-Chat* is particularly interesting in this connexion because it shows Cibber, with an audacity which must have infuriated his enemies, making good-humoured capital out of his own unpopularity. The epilogue is supposed to be extempore. 'No one advancing to the Audience for the Epilogue, Mr. Booth applies to Mrs. Oldfield.'

Mr. *Booth.*   Madam! are n't you to speak the Epilogue?

Mrs. *Old.*   Not I, Sir.

Mr. *Booth.*	Wilks!
Mr. *Wilks.*	If I do, I'm a Dog.
Mr. *Booth.*	Who has it then?
Mrs. *Old.*	I fancy, Cibber.
Mr. *Booth.*	Hay!
Mr. *Wilks.*	The likeliest Man, because he's out o'

th' way.

Mr. *Booth.*	I see him squabbling with the Author

yonder.

O! here he comes.

Mr. *Cibber.*	(*Entring.*) Was ever such a blunder?
Mr. *Wilks.*	The Matter, pray?
Mr. *Cibber.*	These Authors are

such Elves:

Ours thought we found all Epilogues

our selves:

And so the Play has none.

Mr. *Booth.*	What shall we do?
Mrs. *Oldfield.*	Let Cibber speak Extempore.
Mr. *Cibber.*	Why not you?
Mrs. *Old.*	Had I your Wit and Front, Sweet Sir,

I might.

Mr. *Cibber.*	Madam—I've nothing in my Head.
Mrs. *Old.*	You're right:

For faith! I never thought you had—

Good Night.

It is not a very telling hit, but Cibber was compelled to confess to the audience,

She knew at least,
Abusing me wou'd be a standing Jest.

Cibber paid for this unpopularity in several ways. His acting, particularly in tragedy parts, was often hissed, his plays were howled down, his benefit nights were neglected, and his character was abused in every coffee-house and newspaper in London. On one occasion at least, the first performance of his comedy *The Provok'd Husband*, his life was even in some danger. 'Oranges,' we are told, 'Apples, Turnips, etc., flew at your devoted Head from the Galleries, and among the rest of their Artillery a Stone, which put you, as well it might, into a sudden Tremor.'

What is the explanation of the animosity Cibber provoked on almost every side? It was principally, I think, due to that quality in him which his enemies called his insolence, his brazenness, his unabashedness, his impenetrability, but which a more democratic age will call independence. At a time when an actor was expected to kowtow to the aristocracy and to flatter the public, Cibber did neither. There are many anecdotes, often recorded by his enemies, which show that he refused to be overawed by mere rank or mere authority. On one occasion he was told by the profligate Duke of Wharton that he expected to see him hanged or beggared very soon. 'By God,' Cibber retorted with spirit, 'if I had your Grace's Politicks and Morals, you might expect both.' And Dennis records, with the outraged horror of a snob, that on another occasion Cibber refused to act 'one poor Comedy' even at the solicitation of 'Three Peers of England, a Duke and two Earls'. Cibber's character was certainly far from perfect: he was a reckless gamester (a trait inherited from his luckless and talented father), he was selfish and conceited, he was often too free with his sarcasms; but he deserves the credit of the moral courage which this quality of independence implied and necessitated.

No one, not even Pope, denied Cibber's talents. Steele praised him repeatedly, until they finally quarrelled, in all his numerous periodicals; Swift is said to have sat up all night to read the *Apology*; and his wit was the admiration of Brett and Maynwaring,

Pelham and Chesterfield.   In his later years he was
the darling of Will's and White's.   ' I remember to
have seen him,' Erskine Baker wrote, ' when a-midst
a circle of persons, not one of whom perhaps had
attained to the third part of his age, yet has Mr. Cibber,
by his easy good-humour, liveliness of conversation,
and a peculiar happiness he had in telling a story,
been apparently the very life of the company.'   It is
true Cibber was almost the worst poet laureate we
have had.   But the annual New Year and Birthday
Odes, which he turned out with a cynical and mechanical regularity for nearly thirty years, were, at least,
an endless joy to his contemporaries.

> *Strephon.* Colley has tuned again his fife.
> *Thyrsis.*   Has he ? . . . . . . 'slife.
> *Strephon.* Nor is he yet quite out of breath.
> *Thyrsis.*   Not yet ? . . . . . . 'sdeath.

And the unfortunate Colley laughed as much as any
of them.   ' I wrote ', he confessed, ' more to be Fed,
than to be Famous.'   After all, it may be inquired,
how many of the poet laureates of the eighteenth
century did more than that ?

ii

The determination of Cibber's position as a dramatist
is complicated by the fact that a number of the plays
which pass under his name are only his by courtesy.
Pope has described in his first book of *The Dunciad*,

> How, with less reading than makes felons scape,
> Less human genius than God gives an ape,
> Small thanks to France, and none to Rome or Greece,
> A vast, vamp'd, future, old, reviv'd, new piece,

'Twixt Plautus, Fletcher, Shakespear, and Corneille,
Can make a Cibber, Tibbald, or Ozell.

The conjunction of Cibber's name with Theobald's
and Ozell's was a gratuitous insult. At least he never
descended into Grub Street. But the facts, for once,
were on Pope's side. Cibber's tragedies were all,
with two exceptions, 'improvements' upon earlier
plays—*Richard III* and *King John* upon Shakespeare, *Ximena* and *Cinna's Conspiracy* upon Corneille.
And it is the same with the majority of the comedies
and farces. Of the twelve comedies, indeed, only
four—*Love's Last Shift*, *The Careless Husband*, *The
Lady's last Stake*, and the relatively unimportant
Woman's Wit—are in every sense original. It is
upon these plays, and to a lesser degree *The Provok'd
Husband* (an expansion of Vanbrugh's fragmentary
The Journey to London), that his reputation has rested.
They are the most ambitious and on the whole they
are the most successful of his writings. The other
comedies are either translations from Molière or
adaptations, more or less thorough in every instance,
of earlier English plays. In general he has trans-
muted his material, or added to it, with considerable
skill and consistency, and only two of the plays
deserve to be dismissed as plagiarisms. They are *The
Comical Lovers*, a fusion of the comic episodes in three
of Dryden's tragicomedies, and *The Double Gallant*,
which is 'lifted' from Mrs. Centlivre and William
Burnaby. But if there is something of Cibber in almost
all the plays, it is not always prominent and not often
easy to disentangle from the heterogeneous material
in which it is embedded. It is convenient, therefore,
to confine the attention to *Love's Last Shift*, *The
Careless Husband*, *The Lady's Last Stake*, and *The*

Provok'd Husband. It should be added, however, that at any rate *Love makes a Man* and *She wou'd, and She wou'd not* are also well worth reading.

Cibber's début was unusually fortunate. The great Lord Dorset, the Eugenius of Dryden's *Essay of Dramatick Poesy*, pronounced that he had written 'the best First Play that any Author in his Memory had produc'd'. And the audiences were equally enthusiastic. Tom Davies has recorded that the 'joy of unexpected reconcilement, from Loveless's remorse and penitence, spread such an uncommon rapture of pleasure in the audience, that never were spectators more happy in easing their minds by uncommon and repeated plaudits'. *Love's Last Shift; or, the Fool in Fashion*, the play in question, is historically important because it was the first sentimental comedy. It is certain that it provided, as such, a welcome alternative to the monotonous sophistication of the Restoration. It must be confessed, though, that the sentimental passages have not worn well. It is no longer possible for us to appreciate 'the mere moral Delight receiv'd from its Fable' as Cibber's contemporaries did. The didacticism is patently false and factitious. The contrast is too acute between the final, uplifting 'tag',

> And sure the nearest to the Joys above,
> Is the chast Rapture of a Virtuous Love,

and the cynical epilogue which follows immediately:—

> An Honest Rake forego the joys of life !
> His Whores, and Wine ! t'Embrace a Dull Cast Wife ;
> Such out of fashion stuff ! But then agen !
> He's Lewd for above four Acts, Gentlemen !
> For Faith he knew, when once he'd chang'd his Fortune,
> And reform'd his Vice, 'twas Time—to drop the Curtain.

The moral of the play, as we would draw it, is
pointed by Snap, Loveless's faithful but prosaic valet.
'I thank Heav'n, that I have so much Grace left,
that I can repent, when I have no more opportunities
of being wicked.' They were more naïve in 1696.

The hero is Loveless, who is described in the
dramatis personae as of 'a debaucht life, grew weary
of his Wife in six Months, left her, and the Town,
for Debts he did not care to pay; and having spent
the last part of his Estate beyond Sea, returns to
England in a very mean condition'. The heroine
is the still affectionate Amanda. A plot is made to
reconcile them, and he is introduced to Amanda in
the dark as to a desirable mistress. He falls head
over heels in love with his unknown charmer and
has the good grace, when he discovers who she is, to
admit the error of his ways and implore his wife's
forgiveness. A mawkish scene of reconciliation brings
the play to an end. In his unregenerate days Loveless is a very spirited character, as racy and as cynical
as Dorimant himself. The audience must have known
the type well. He is the realist who knows that
'a Wife is an Eternal Apple-tree, after a pull or two
you are sure to set your Teeth on Edge'. He is the
sceptic who observes with the gusto of the young
rakes in Dryden's comedies a 'jolly Red-Nos'd Parson,
at Three a Clock in the Morning, Belch out Invectives
against late Hours, and hard Drinking'. But as the
play progresses his animation decreases, until finally
we find him delivering himself to Amanda in this
fashion :—

> *Lov.* I have wrong'd you. Oh! rise! basely wrong'd
> you! and can I see your Face?
> *Am.* One kind, one pitying look cancels those wrongs

for ever: and oh! forgive my fond presuming passion;
for from my Soul I pardon and forgive you all: all, all
but this, the greatest, your unkind Delay of Love.

Lov. Oh! seal my pardon with thy trembling Lips,
while with this tender Grasp of fond reviving Love
I seize my Bliss and stifle all thy wrongs for ever.

(*Embraces her.*)

Am. No more; I'le wash away their memory in tears of
flowing Joy.

Lov. Oh thou hast rouz'd me from my deep Lethargy
of Vice! For hitherto my Soul has been enslav'd to
loose Desires, to vain deluding Follies, and shadows of
substantial bliss: but now I wake with joy to find my
Rapture Real.— . . . Oh! why have I so long been blind
to the Perfections of thy Mind and Person! Not knowing thee a Wife, I found thee Charming beyond the
wishes of Luxurious Love. . . . Oh! I have wander'd
like a benighted wretch, and lost myself in Lifes Unpleasing Journey.

It was with an eye on such passages as this that
Pope ridiculed Cibber's 'prose on stilts' and 'poetry
fall'n lame'. To-day, however, the difficulty is not
so much the wretchedness of the writing, as the
psychological *volte-face*. There was nothing in what
preceded to prepare us for Loveless's conversion; there
is nothing in what follows to justify it. It is spectacular,
and therefore theatrically effective; but it is recklessly
untrue to life; it is not even true to what we should
like life to be. An interesting feature of the speeches
is the blank verse which is concealed in the prose.
The final sentence might as well be printed,

Oh! I have wander'd like a benighted wretch,
And lost myself in Lifes Unpleasing Journey.

The verse is explained by the fact that Cibber was
attempting to introduce into comedy the pathetic

elements which Otway and Southerne had exploited
in *The Orphan* and *The Fatal Marriage*, and unconsciously he incorporated with the material of these
tragedies their technique. It was not until much
later that he was to discover 'a great deal of Puerility
and frothy Stage-Language' in these scenes.

The minor characters of the comedy, though they
were less original, are more credible than Loveless
and Amanda. The younger Worthy is an agreeable
rake and his *inamorata* Narcissa (who is of the opinion
that 'it looks too Credulous and Easy in a Woman to
Encourage a Man before he has sigh'd himself to a
Skeleton') is a delightful jilt. But head and shoulders
above the others is Cibber's own part, 'the Fool in
Fashion' of the subtitle, that man of mode, the
inimitable Sir Novelty Fashion. It is, we learn,
Sir Novelty's ambition to be 'a true Original, the
very Pink of Fashion', and he is an industriously
inane labourer in his vocation:

> Sir *Nov.* Then you must know my Coach, and
> Equipage are as well known, as my self; and since the
> conveniency of two Play-Houses I have a better Oppor-
> tunity of shewing them; For between every Act—
> Whisk—I am gone from one to th' other—Oh! what
> Pleasure 'tis at a good Play, to go out before half an
> Act's done!
>   *Nar.* Why at a good Play?
>   Sir *Nov.* O! Madam it looks Particular, and gives
> the whole Audience an Opportunity of turning upon me
> at once: Then do they conclude I have some Extra-
> ordinary Business, or a Fine Woman to go to at least:
> And then again it shews my Contempt of what the
> dull Town think their chiefest Diversion: But if I do
> stay a Play out, I always set with my Back to the Stage.
>   *Nar.* Why so Sir?

Sir *Nov.* Then every Body will imagine I have been
tired with it before; or that I am jealous who talks
to who in the Kings Box. And thus, Madam, do
I take more pains to preserve a Publick Reputation,
than ever any Lady took after the Small-Pox, to recover
her Complexion.

Sir Novelty employs on occasion a certain affected
modesty. 'Pray Madam,' he asks Narcissa when
they first meet, 'how do I looke to day? What,
Cursedly? I'll warrant with a more Hellish Complexion, than a Stale Actress at a Rehearsal —.' It
deceives nobody and it is not meant to. We are all
of us certain that he is much too careful a general of
effects to have overlooked so important an outwork
as the complexion. He is, indeed, impeccably eccentric in every detail. The buttons he wears on his
coat are as large as saucers—'not above three Inches
Diameter', he confesses with the same ironical mock-
modesty. And his sleeves, at a period when sleeves
stopped at the elbows, come over his wrists and almost
cover the knuckles. He is as exquisite in his oaths
as he is in his dress. 'Burn me,' he swears, 'Stop
my Vitals,' 'Strike me dumb.' It is his greatest pride
that he 'was the first Person in England that was
complemented with the name of Beau', and he is so
fully aware of the dignity of the title that he intends
'to write a Play, where my Chiefest Character shall
be a down-right English Booby that affects to be a
Beau, without either Genius or Foreign Education,
and to call it in Imitation of another famous Comedy,
He wou'd if he cou'd'. Evidently Sir Novelty had
studied his predecessors, the Sir Fopling Flutter of
Etherege and the Sir Courtly Nice of Crowne in
particular; but he is not, as it has been asserted, their

duplicate. Sir Fopling and Sir Courtly were born fools, nature's asses; but Sir Novelty is a fool carefully and conscientiously self-made. He has brains, and his fopperies and affectations are merely a deliberate experiment in self-advertisement.

The most successful scene of the play is in the second act. Narcissa, the younger Worthy, and Sir Novelty are on the stage, and the gentlemen, each in his own way, are making love to the lady. Sir Novelty's wooing takes the form of a recitation of his own achievements in the world of fashion. 'The Cravat-string,' he concludes in a final summary of his career, 'the Garter, the Sword-knot, the Centurine, the Bardash, the Steinkirk, the large Button, the long Sleeve, the Plume, and full Peruque, were all created, cry'd down, or revived by me.' The more tactful Worthy indulges himself only in a catalogue of the charms of Narcissa. 'Why, Madam,' he begins, 'I have observed several particular Qualities in your Ladyship, that I have perfectly ador'd you for, as the Majestick toss of your Head—Your obliging Bow'd Curtesie — your Satyrical Smile — Your blushing Laugh—your Demure Look—the careless Tye of your Hood—the Genteel flirt of your Fan—The designed Accident in your letting fall, and your agreeable manner of receiving it from him that takes it up.' A stage direction explains that all the time 'What he speaks she imitates in dumb shew', and finally the two gentlemen 'both offer to take up her Fan, and in striving Y. Worthy pushes Sir Novelty on his Back'. There is something of the vulgarity of farce in the final rough-and-tumble, but with that exception the scene is composed with an admirable lightness and certainty of touch. It is reminiscent of Etherege

and is a refreshing contrast to the turgid rhapsodies
of Loveless and Amanda.

The Careless Husband is *Love's Last Shift* without
its defects of taste.   The fundamental confusion remains; it was beyond Cibber's power to reconcile
the artificial values of the Restoration comedies and
the ethics of 'sentimentalism'.   But the failure is not
obvious.   The juxtaposition of the scenes of sentiment
and high comedy is managed with tact and discretion.
There is very little of that forcing the note and over-
emphasis which are so disconcerting in the earlier
play.   In one or two of the episodes there is even
an elusive suggestion that the contradiction has been
resolved.   The *dramatis personae* are only seven.
There are three gentlemen of rank and fashion—
Lord Morelove, Lord Foppington, and Sir Charles
Easy; there are three ladies *à la mode*—Lady Betty
Modish, Lady Easy, and Lady Graveairs; and there
is Mrs. Edging the abigail.   The theme of the play,
the reconciliation of an estranged husband and wife,
is the same as in *Love's Last Shift*, but its treatment
is at once more mature, more plausible, and more
subtle. Sir Charles Easy is a dissolute, and yet good-
hearted, man of quality.   He describes himself not
unjustly as ' A loose Unheeding Wretch, Absent in
all I do, Civil, and as often Rude without design,
Unseasonably Thoughtful, Easy to a Fault, and in
my Best of Praise but Carelessly Good Natur'd '.
The tolerant and sensible Lady Easy winks at his
intrigues with Edging and Lady Graveairs, and lives
in the hope of reclaiming him by never upbraiding
him with his infidelities.   Her opportunity comes
when she discovers Sir Charles and Edging fast asleep

together in their bedroom. At the first shock of surprise her patience almost fails her.

> I'll throw this Vizor of my Patience off:
> Now wake him in his Guilt,
> And Barefac'd Front him with my Wrongs,

But she recollects herself in time :—

> Perhaps
> The Fault's in me, and Nature has not Form'd
> Me with the Thousand little Requisites
> That Warms the Heart to Love—

and then she notices that he has not got his wig on. Perhaps he will catch cold,

> Who knows, while thus Expos'd to the unwholesome Air But Heav'n offended may o'ertake his Crime, and in some languishing Distemper leave him a severe Example of his violated Laws—Forbid it Mercy, and forbid it Love. This may prevent it.

And so the stage direction comes, ' Takes her Steinkirk from her Neck, and lays it gently over his Head '. Lady Easy's forbearance is rewarded when Sir Charles wakes up and, recognizing the steinkirk, is overwhelmed with remorse.

> Did I not see my Wife wear this to Day ?—Death ! she can't have been here sure ! It cou'd not be a Jealousie that Brought her home—for my coming was Accidental—so too, I fear, might hers.—How careless have I been ?—Not to secure the Door neither—'Twas Foolish—It must be so ! She certainly has seen me here Sleeping with her Woman—If so, How low an Hypocrite to her must that sight have Prov'd me ?

There is finally an ample and generous reconciliation. The steinkirk scene, as it may be called, is the climax of the play. It is not, however, by any means the most successful scene in it. The psychology is credible, but the writing is miserable—now in Sir Charles's soliloquy 'prose on stilts', now in Lady Easy's 'poetry fall'n lame'. It is one of the curious features of the sentimental comedies of the eighteenth century that the writing always deteriorates as the emotions are intensified. The earlier scenes, where Lady Easy, patient and heart-broken, puts a smiling face on the infidelities of the somewhat shamefaced Sir Charles, are infinitely more natural and more affecting.

> Sir *Cha*. Are you then really very happy, my Dear?
> La. *Ea*. Why shou'd you question it? [*Smiling on him.*
> Sir *Cha*. Because I fancy I am not so good to you as I should be.
> La. *Ea*. Pshah!
> Sir *Cha*. Nay, the Duce take me if I don't really confess my self so bad, that I have often wonder'd how any Woman of your Sense, Rank and Person, could think it worth her while to have so many useless good Qualities.
> La. *Ea*. Fie, my Dear.
> Sir *Cha*. By my Soul I'm serious.
> La. *Ea*. I can't boast of my good Qualities, nor if I could, do I believe you think 'em useless.
> Sir *Cha*. Nay, I submit to you—Don't you find 'em so? Do you perceive that I am one Tittle the better Husband for your being so good a Wife?
> La. *Ea*. Pshah! you Jest with me.
> Sir *Cha*. I don't really—Tell me truly, was you never Jealous of me?
> La. *Ea*. Did I ever give you any sign of it?
> Sir *Cha*. Um—that's true—but do you really think I never gave you Occasion?
> La. *Ea*. That's an odd Question—but suppose you had?
> Sir *Cha*. Why then, what good has your Virtue done

you, since all the good Qualities of it could not keep me
to your self?

    La. *Ea.* What occasion have you given me to suppose
I have not kept you to my self?

The dialogue is not showy, but it rings true. It was
in delicate analyses of this sort that Cibber's ' sentimentalism ' was most properly employed.

The coquettish Lady Betty Modish (a portrait
from the life, it is said, of Mrs. Oldfield the actress)
provides an admirable foil to Lady Easy. She is
a bouncing, high-spirited creature, clever and good-
natured, but anxious only to appear fashionably cynical
and affected. She comes in quite out of breath, girl-
ishly excited about the new scarf she has just received
from London. ' 'Tis all Extravagance both in Mode
and Fancy ; my Dear, I believe there's Six Thousand
Yards of Edging in it—Then such an Enchanting
Slope from the Elbow—something so New, so Lively,
so Noble, so Coquet and Charming.' The next
minute she is the *grande dame*, cynical and assured.
' Pshaw !' she is telling Lady Easy, with a perhaps
intentional reminiscence of Millamant, ' will any
thing a Man says make a Woman less agreeable ?
Will his Talking spoil ones Complexion, or put ones
Hair out of order ? ' Lady Betty's heart is with the
faithful, but rather heavy, Lord Morelove, and the
curtain goes down upon their engagement. But until
the last moment she flirts persistently with Lord
Foppington, and their billing and cooing, with the
raillery they expend upon the unfortunate Morelove,
provide some of the most attractive things in the
play :—

    La. *Bet.* Sincerity in Love is as much out of Fashion
as sweet Snuff; No Body takes it now.

L. *Fop.* O ! no Mortal, Madam, unless it be here and there a Squire, that's making his lawful Court to the Cherry-cheek Charms of my Lord Bishop's great fat Daughter in the Country.

Or again :—

L. *Fop.* I observe two People of Extreme Condition can no sooner Grow Particular, but the Multitude of Both Sexes are Immediately Up, and think their Properties invaded.
La. *Bet.* Odious Multitude.
L. *Fop.* Perish that Canaille.

Lord Foppington is the Sir Novelty Fashion of *Love's Last Shift* (he had been raised to the peerage by Vanbrugh in *The Relapse*). He is more accomplished and more civilized than he was when only a commoner. His taste has improved, his self-sufficiency is less pronounced, and he has developed his eccentricities into a consistent philosophy of nonchalance. 'If a Man don't mind a Box on the Ear in a fair Struggle with a Fresh Country Girl, why the Devil shou'd he be concern'd at an Impertinent Frown for an Attack upon a Woman of Quality.' With the passage of the years he has become more of an amorist, though he has yet to fall into the indignity of being in love. His 'affairs' are still part of a campaign of self-advertisement. 'I think', he confides to Morelove, 'the Reputation is the most Inviting Part of an Amour'. The secret of Lord Foppington's charm is the air with which he carries everything off; he has the grand manner. It may only be to refer to his horses—'Foppington's Long-Tails are known in every Road in England'. Or it may be to save his honour in a difficult situation :—

L. *Fop.* By all that's Infamous she Jilted me.

L. *Mo.* How! Jilt you?

L. *Fop.* Ay, Death's Curse, she Jilted me.

L. *Mo.* Pray let's hear.

L. *Fop.* For when I was pretty well convinc'd she had a Mind to me, I one Day made her a Hint of an Appointment; upon which, with an Insolent frown in her face (that made her look as ugly as the Devil) she told me, that if ever I came thither again, her Lord should know that she had forbidden me the House before; ha! ha! Did you ever hear of such a Slut?

Sir *Cha.* Intollerable!

L. *Mo.* But how did her Answer agree with you?

L. *Fop.* Passionately well—For I star'd full in her Face, and Busted out a laughing, at which she turn'd upon her Heel, gave a Crack with her Fan like a Coach-whip, and Bridl'd out of the Room with the Air and Complexion of an Incens'd Turkey-Cock.

He is, indeed, at his best in defeat. The humiliation of the final and unexpected surrender of Lady Betty to Lord Morelove only spurs him to greater heights of self-complacency. 'I am struck Dumb with the Deliberation of her Assurance; and do not Positively remember, that the Non Challence of my Temper ever had so Bright an Occasion to shew it self before.' And he goes on to reassure Lady Betty. 'Madam, I have lost a thousand Fine Women in my time; But never had the Ill Manners to be out of Humour with any one for refusing me, since I was Born.' In these moments the *sangfroid* of Lord Foppington becomes almost heroic, a gesture magnificent in its absurdity. We have lost the coxcomb in another Don Quixote, a superb and imperturbable knight-errant of the drawing-rooms.

The Lady's last Stake, or, the Wife's Resentment is a pendant to *The Careless Husband*, and therefore to

Love's Last Shift. The moral of the earlier plays had been that a generous and tolerant wife was the only remedy for an erring husband. In *The Lady's last Stake* the moral is still enforced, but by the exactly opposite means of depicting the conduct, not to be imitated, but to be avoided. Lord Wronglove is a good-natured, self-indulgent egoist who amuses himself with the 'Baby-fac'd' little Miss Notable, though his heart is still with his wife. He is the Sir Charles Easy of the play. On the other hand Lady Wronglove, in contrast to Lady Easy, is proud, cold, and implacably virtuous. She dogs her husband in his amours, and her reproaches become irritants which increase instead of repressing his follies. The contrast is explicitly emphasized in the dialogue between Lady Wronglove and Hartshorn in the fourth Act.

> La. *Wrong.* What is the Play to Day?
>
> Mrs. *Harts.* The — the — Husband, something — the Careful Husband, I think, Madam.
>
> La. *Wrong.* The Careful; the Careless Husband, you mean sure—tho' I never saw it.
>
> Mrs. *Harts.* Yes, yes, Madam—it's that Play, that my Lady Wear-breeches hates so, that I saw once, Madam—where there's a Lady that comes in, and catches her Husband fast asleep with her own Woman, and then takes her Steinkirk off her Neck, and then goes softly to him—
>
> La. *Wrong.* And strangles him in his Sleep?
>
> Mrs. *Harts.* No, Madam.
>
> La. *Wrong.* Oh, strangles the Woman.
>
> Mrs. *Harts.* No, Madam, she only lays it gently over his Head, for fear he shou'd catch Cold, and so steals out of the Room, without so much as offering to wake him.

La. *Wrong*. Horrid! And what becomes of the poor spirited Creature?

Mrs. *Harts*. O! Madam, when the Gentleman wakes, and finds that his Lady has been there without taking any notice of it to him, he grows so sham'd of his Wickedness, and so sensible of her Vertue, that he afterwards proves the civilest Gentleman, and the best Husband in the World to her.

La. *Wrong*. Foh! were I an Husband, a Wife with such a tame enduring Spirit wou'd make me scorn her, or, at best, but sleep at her groveling Vertue.

Lord and Lady Wronglove are still fond of each other, but they are too proud to admit it, too influenced by the trifling squabbles of every day even to realize it. A divorce would be the only possible solution of their difficulties in this world. Cibber takes his characters to the edge of it, only to allow a convenient *deus ex machina* then to appear in the person of a kindly busybody, Sir Friendly Moral, who miraculously reconciles everybody. It was not the conclusion required by the moral, and it spoils the play. Cibber's real achievement was to have shown that life, even in the eighteenth century, was not a matter of great moments, but a daily round of nervous irritation, petty quarrels, and insignificant injuries. The fundamental moral of the play was Laforgue's,

Ah! que la Vie est quotidienne.

For the moment Cibber was the precursor of Tchehov and the happy ending is irrelevant and illogical.

The Lady's last Stake is the most serious of Cibber's plays. Primarily it is a comedy of ideas, a problem play in embryo. But there is a lighter side to it too. There is the impudent and high-spirited Mrs. Conquest;

there is Lord George Brilliant, an amusing coxcomb
and a rake of distinction. They are good fun, both
of them. Lord George, with his new chariot, 'positively the prettiest that ever roll'd in the Rear of six
Horses', and his cynical epigrams, is a kind of reproduction of Lord Foppington. He is the most accomplished phrase-maker in the play, and he all but
overwhelms Miss Notable with modish metaphors
and similes. 'I gad', he tells her, 'the Child's
a Bars length in Experience above the stoutest of her
Sex'. And to add force to the asseveration that 'her
Person's quite out of my Goust' he concludes, 'nor
have I any more Concern about it than I have to
know who will be the next King of Poland, or who
is the true Original of Strops for Razors'.¹ The
most vital person in the play is little Miss Notable
herself. She is alarmingly alive, as exuberantly full
of animal spirits as Vanbrugh's Hoyden or Congreve's
Miss Prue, and as wanton and suspicious as any of her
elders and betters. She has already acquired the
authentic Restoration philosophy of love. 'Now
I think', she maintains, 'a young Creature, that
fairly trusts to her Heels, and leads you twenty, or
thirty couple of brisk young Fellows after her Helter
Skelter, over Hills, Hedges, Boggs, and Ditches, has
ten times a fairer Chance for her Life ; and if she is
taken at last, I hold Twenty to one among any
People of Taste, they'll say she's better Meat by half.'
And she is full of extraordinary slang. One of the
letters she writes to Lord Wronglove runs, 'I Won't
beg your Pardon for not coming Yesterday, because it

¹ A wordy warfare was being conducted in the newspapers by
the rival vendors of the latest in strops. It was still raging when
Swift was writing the *Journal to Stella*.

was not my Fault, but indeed I'm sorry I could not. To be short, old Teizer smoaks the Business, poss— For he watch'd me all Day as if he had been in love with me himself: But you may depend upon me this Afternoon, about five at the same Place, till when, dear Dismal, adieu.' The 'old Teizer' was the elderly and respectable Sir Friendly Moral.

The Provok'd Husband is based on and incorporates Vanbrugh's brilliant fragment, *The Journey to London*, and its most successful scenes are not Cibber's. The effective conclusion, however, is entirely his. Vanbrugh had intended the husband to turn his frivolous wife out of doors. In the interests of sentiment Cibber reforms her and arranges a reconciliation between the husband and wife, which is comparable to those in *The Careless Husband*, *Love's Last Shift*, and *The Lady's last Stake*. The difference is an illuminating indication of the essential divergence between the didacticism of the seventeenth century and the 'sentimentalism' of the eighteenth century. The provoked husband in Cibber's play is the sensible and sober Lord Townly, and the provoking wife is the flighty and neurotic, but always adorable, Lady Townly. The climax comes with the exhaustion of Lord Townly's patience. 'As the Lord Townly's Wife', he begins, ' you have had every thing a fond Husband could bestow, and (to our mutual Shame I speak it) more than happy Wives desire—But those Indulgencies must end! State, Eqipage, and Splendor but ill become the Vices that misuse 'em.—The decent Necessaries of Life shall be supply'd —but not one Article of Luxury !' And then, in the most sentimental but not in its context the least convincing passage of the

play, Townly turns to his friend Manly. 'O Manly!
look there! turn back thy Thoughts with me, and
witness to my growing Love! there was a time when
I believ'd that Form incapable of Vice, or of Decay!
There I propos'd the Partner of an easy Home! There!
I, for ever, hop'd to find a cheerful Companion, an
agreeable Intimate, a faithful Friend, a useful Help-
mate, and a tender Mother—But oh! how bitter now
the Disappointment!' The scene is worth comparing
with the almost identical situation in *The Lady's last
Stake*, but the solution of the later play—Lady Townly
repents and is forgiven—is the more plausible, because
it has dispensed with the *deus ex machina* of Sir
Friendly Moral.

It is curious that the central situation in Cibber's
more important comedies is always the same. There
are differences of detail in the relations of Loveless to
Amanda, of Sir Charles to Lady Easy, and of Lord
Wronglove and Lord Townly to their wives; but
the problem, the reconciliation of a couple who have
drifted apart, and the solution, to forgive and forget,
do not change. It is his principal contribution to
sentimental comedy. Was it a coincidence? Was
it the wordly wisdom of repeating a formula that had
proved popular? Or was it a vicarious atonement
for his own delinquencies? It is tempting to see
behind the Amandas and the Lady Easy's a sorely
tried and perhaps not sufficiently resigned Mrs.
Cibber.[1]

---

[1] Nothing seems to be known about Mrs. Cibber, except that
she 'performed in a masterly Manner on a Harpsichord' and possessed 'every personal Charm that could render a Female amiable
and attractive'.

iii

Cibber was a professional dramatist, and the adaptations of Molière, Fletcher, Dryden, Vanbrugh, and the others which he perpetrated were a natural part of the dramatic profession as it was understood in the eighteenth century. It was not his object to improve his predecessors, but to popularize them, and the invidious comparisons should not be pressed upon him. It is obvious that his plays are without the *vis comica* of Molière and Vanbrugh, and the graces of style which mark even the failures of Fletcher and Dryden. But the objection is irrelevant. Cibber would have admitted as much himself. It is fairer to take him on his own level. On that level he is a competent and attractive dramatist of the second order : more competent than Crowne, more attractive than Shadwell. He has that indefinable sense of the theatre which is only possessed by a good actor ; he knows better than any of his contemporaries the secrets of construction. And then he has a genuine flair for the comedy of high life, for the antics and affectations of the modish and always slightly ridiculous gentleman and lady of quality. As for his pert servants, his boors and his hoydens—the Snaps, the Mass Johnnies and the Miss Notables—he is at least clever enough to be able to reproduce in them the conventional figures of Restoration comedy. Moreover, he can turn a phrase with the best of them. Consider this portrait of Morelove's in *The Careless Husband* of a young exquisite :—

—the Pert Coxcomb that's just come to a small Estate, and a great Periwig—he that Sings himself among the Women—What d'ye call him ?—He won't speak to a Gentleman when a Lord's in Company—you always see him with a Cane dangling at his Button, his Breast open, no Gloves, one Eye tuck'd under his Hat, and a Tooth-pick—Startup! That's his Name.

Or take the simile with which Lord Wronglove welcomes his wife as she comes in from the rain 'in a Hood and Scarf, and her Petticoat pinn'd' :—

In just such a Trim have I seen a trigg'd up Drury-Lane-Gentlewoman come daggled along from Market with a comfortable Pound of Beef-stakes upon a Scuer.

Trigged up, daggled, comfortable—it is an exquisite vignette, worthy almost of Congreve.

But in the eighteenth century it was thought that Cibber was something more than a competent, successful dramatist of the second rank. Defoe's grandson, David Erskine Baker, was of the opinion that 'the English Stage' is 'more obliged to Mr. Cibber for a Fund of rational Entertainment, than to any dramatic Writer the Nation has produced, Shakespeare only excepted'. *The Careless Husband* was extolled to the skies. Samuel Derrick (that Derrick for whom Johnson 'had a kindness') considered that it was ' not only the best Comedy in the English, but in any other language', and Baker agreed that it contained 'the most elegant Dialogue, and the most perfect Knowledge of the Manners of Persons in real high Life extant in any dramatic Piece that has yet appear'd in any Language whatever'. Voltaire complimented 'le mary negligent' in the *Lettres Philosophiques*, and even Pope, with his life-long antipathy to Cibber, has commended the play in the *Epistle to Augustus*:—

All this may be; the People's Voice is odd,
It is, and it is not, the voice of God.

To Gammer Gurton if it give the bays,
And yet deny the Careless Husband praise,
Or say our Fathers never broke a rule;
Why then, I say, the Public is a fool.[1]

They are judgements which must seem utterly fantastic to us; but they are not inexplicable. Cibber was a pioneer. It was to him the century was indebted for ' the reformation of the stage'. ' The first comedy', says Tom Davies, 'acted since the Restoration, in which was preserved purity of manners and decency of language, with due respect to the honour of the marriage-bed, was Colley Cibber's *Love's Last Shift*'. One cannot get away from Cibber's morality. It is praised everywhere, even by the most unlikely people. Cibber himself was never tired of informing his readers that a ' Play without a just Moral, is a poor and mercenary Undertaking,' or that the ' Best Criticks have long, and justly complain'd, that the Coarseness of most Characters in our late Comedies have been unfit Entertainments for People of Quality, especially the Ladies'. He expatiates upon the theme in the *Apology*:

when I was warmly engag'd upon a Subject entirely new, I only thought it a good Subject, when it seem'd worthy of an abler Pen than my own, and might prove as useful to the Hearer, as profitable to myself; Therefore, whatever any of my productions might want of Skill, Learning, Wit or Humour, or however unqualify'd I might be to instruct others, who so ill-govern'd myself: Yet such Plays (entirely my own) were not

---

[1] The one dissentient voice was Congreve's. 'Cibber has produced a play', he wrote to Joseph Keally, 'consisting of fine gentlemen and fine conversation altogether; which the ridiculous town for the most part likes: but there are some that know better'.

wanting, at least, in what our most admired Writers seem'd to neglect, and without which I cannot allow the most taking Play to be intrinsically good, or to be a Work upon which a Man of Sense and Probity should value himself: I mean when they do not as well *prodesse*, as *delectare*, give Profit with Delight!

How far, one wonders, was it sincere? It is difficult to believe, as one can with Steele, that Cibber's didacticism came from the heart. It is too cold-blooded, too factitiously 'high-faluting'. The real Cibber is revealed, not in these stilted scenes of reconciliation, but in the 'luscious' dialogue with which almost all his plays are filled. Some of the additions he has made to Mrs. Centlivre in *The Double Gallant* and to Fletcher in *Love makes a Man* are inexcusable. Here is a passage from *She wou'd, and She wou'd not*:—

what pleasure 'twou'd be to have her steal out of her Bed in a sweet Moonshine Night, to hear her come pat! pat! pat! along in her Slippers, with nothing but a thin silk Night-gown loose about her, and in this Tempting Dress, to have her jump into my Arms breathless with Fear, her fainting Bosom close to mine; then to stifle her with Kisses, and curl myself about her smooth, warm Limbs, that breathe an healing Odour from their Pores enough to make the Senses ach, or Fancy mad!

It is a pretty picture, but was it the writing of a sincere moralist? It is not extraordinary that Cibber's contemporaries sometimes contrasted his practice with his professions. There is a story that 'Mrs. Porter, upon reading a part in which Cibber had painted virtue in the strongest and most lively colours, asked him how it came to pass, that a man, who could draw such admirable portraits of goodness, should yet live as if he were a stranger to it?'

Cibber's answer, a compound of cynicism and hypocrisy, is most illuminating. 'Madam,' said Colley, 'the one is absolutely necessary, the other is not'.

The fact is that Cibber's 'sentimentalism' was not primarily ethical, but psychological. It was the antithesis, that is to say, of Steele's. The ambition of Steele, and his successors like Kelly and Cumberland, was limited to arousing in the audience 'A generous Pity of a painted Woe'. Cibber was more interested in disclosing and defining the subtler shades of character (though they might be shades cast by an ethical problem). The difference may be illustrated by a consideration of the contrasting 'sensibilities' of Nivelle de la Chaussée and Marivaux. It is Marivaux, the Marivaux of *Marianne* or *Le Legs*, whom Cibber suggests. *The Careless Husband* is, of course, inferior as psychology, inferior in *finesse* and in persistency; but the inferiority was not, I think, essential. It was due to the accident that Cibber was born in England. In the natural quality of their talents they were probably not far apart. Cibber was unfortunate because he was born at once too early and too late. If he had been thirty years older he would now be with Etherege; if he had been thirty years younger he might have effected the revolution in the drama which Richardson effected in the novel. His allegiance was divided between the two schools of artifice and naturalism. He has his place in both schools; but his place must be in the second rank of either, because he had become the dramatist of a compromise—the compromise which is known in literary history as 'genteel comedy'.

III

RICHARD STEELE

i

IT is impossible to think of Steele except in conjunction with Addison; they, rather than Beaumont and Fletcher, are the *Dioscuri* of English literature. But the two friends, though they were at school and at Oxford together, though they collaborated so successfully that it is often impossible to distinguish between their writings, were oddly dissimilar and fundamentally, I think, incompatible. The friendship, long before the final breach over the Peerage Bill, was always a little artificial; tainted, on Steele's side by hero-worship, on Addison's by condescension.

Addison is, to-day more than ever, an enigma. It is probable, indeed, that we shall never know the whole truth about his relations either with Pope or with Swift. But at least we have outgrown the open-mouthed fascination which he exercised upon Macaulay. We have learnt to look with more suspicion upon one side of his character—the side which is represented by Young's anecdote of the dying Addison summoning to the deathbed his disreputable step-son to see 'in what peace a Christian can die'. We can feel that the note is false, that it is not the grand manner but a theatrical simulation of it; the gesture almost, with a change of key and situation, of a Tartufe or a Pecksniff. But if Addison the man is still obscure, Addison the writer does not present many difficulties to the modern reader. With Steele the position is

exactly reversed. 'Dear Dick Steele', 'the sentimental debauchee' (the phrases are Swinburne's), is
more familiar to us, as a human being, than any of
his contemporaries. We can visualize him, with his
immense Ramillies wig, his shining, swarthy skin, his
brilliant brown eyes, and his irresistible Irish brogue—
'A Shape', growled an enemy, 'like the Picture of
somebody over a Farmer's Chimney, a short Chin, a
short Nose, a short Forehead, a broad flat Face, and
a dusky Countenance'. We can sympathize with his
frank and generous ways, his magnificent enthusiasms
and desperate despondencies. We can forgive him,
though Lady Steele could not, if he is often in liquor
and always in debt. We can bear with him, though
Swift might not, if he does not keep his appointments,
'nor never did twice, since I knew him'. He is a
Goldsmith *manqué*, rather more stupid and decidedly
coarser, but infinitely charming. It is Steele's volu-
minous and extraordinarily unequal writings which are
less easy to 'place'.

His range was comparatively narrow. The best
passages in the essays and the best scenes in the
comedies are all, in a complimentary sense, 'sentimental'; that is to say, the sentiment did not pass
over into sentimentality. They have the freshness,
the naïve charm, the delicacy and sincerity, which
we associate with the 'innocents' of literature, the
Dekkers and Herricks and Clares. They perpetuate,
in a heightened form, the lucid, untroubled, unsophis-
ticated experiences of childhood. 'You like to see
his enjoyment', Thackeray has said of Steele, 'as you
like to see the glee of a box full of children at the
pantomime'. It is not an accident, I fancy, that the
most famous essay in *The Tatler*—that on his father's

death—was a recollection of Steele's own childhood. The essay is entirely characteristic because, with all its pathos, it is not without the suggestion of humour, that flavour of the mock-heroic, which invariably accompanied him, whatever his theme might be, when he was most himself.

Unfortunately lapses of taste and lapses of power are not less characteristic of Steele's writings. I do not mean the occasional indecencies, which are never furtive and were probably altogether unconscious. (Steele was never 'refined', instinctively chastened, like Addison.) I mean the insincerity and the stupidity which go with the sentimentality and the didacticism, and make the one nauseating and the other tedious. Perhaps it would be possible to consider this sentimentality and this didacticism as respectively an excess and a defect of the 'sentiment' which is peculiar to him. They are essentially the penalty exacted by an insufficient assimilation of experience. The humanistic and ethical view of the world, which is characteristic of the eighteenth century, had not *transformed* Steele as in different ways it transformed Addison and Swift. It was only half-digested, and its expression, in consequence, is only partially successful. It was not the arduously acquired philosophy of a lifetime, but a lesson learnt by rote and not by heart; or if by the heart, at least not by the head.

As a dramatist Steele's reputation has suffered, on the whole, by the prominence that is usually given to *The Conscious Lovers*, a play which emphasizes his deficiencies without displaying his qualities. *The Conscious Lovers* is a *reductio ad absurdum* of the sentimental formula. In Hazlitt's celebrated phrase, it is one of 'those do-me-good, lack-a-daisical, whining, make-believe comedies ' which are ' enough to set one to sleep, and where the author tries in vain to be merry and wise in the same breath'. But it should be remembered that this play is separated from Steele's other comedies by some twenty years. It is, comparatively, an old man's play. The freshness and the vivacity which characterize the earlier pieces are strikingly absent from it. To turn from *The Conscious Lovers* to *The Funeral* and *The Tender Husband* is to turn from the 'dotages' of his senility to a world not very different from that contemplated by Isaac Bickerstaff and Mr. Spectator.

ii

In the April of 1701 Steele, then a captain in the Coldstream Guards, published the very characteristic manual of piety which he called *The Christian Hero : An Argument proving that No Principles but those of Religion are sufficient to make a Great Man.* It is an odd little book, its oddest pages being taken up with an ingenious modernization of St. Paul's Epistle to Philemon ; but it is remembered to-day only because, in a roundabout way, it made Steele into a dramatist.[1] *The Christian Hero*, it appears, was a distinct success with the general public, a second edition appearing

---

[1] Actually Steele's first comedy was written while he was still an undergraduate at Oxford. It was burnt by the advice of a candid friend who told him it was worthless. Another comedy called *The Election of Gotham* was planned and perhaps partly written in 1702. The two fragmentary pieces, *The School of Action* and *The Gentleman*, which were printed by Nichols from the manuscripts now in the British Museum, seem to have been written much later. They are not important.

already in July. It was not equally popular with the Captain's brother officers at the Tower. He was 'slighted', he complained later, 'instead of being encouraged, for his Declarations as to Religion', and he was compelled to realize that 'it was now incumbent upon him to enliven his Character'. 'From being thought no undelightful Companion,. he was soon reckoned a disagreeable Fellow.' The rehabilitation of his character was effected by a lively comedy, *The Funeral: or, Grief A-la-mode*, which was completed in October 1701, and brought out at Drury Lane 'with more than expected Success' before the end of the year. 'Nothing', Steele has himself said, 'can make the Town so fond of a Man as a successful Play'.

The plot of *The Funeral* is not without its absurdities. Lord Brumpton has fallen into a 'lethargic slumber' and is supposed, by his friends and family, to be dead. On his recovery he is persuaded by Trusty, the faithful old family retainer, to conceal himself, so that he can discover how his relations are taking the news of his death. The result of what he overhears and oversees is to open his eyes to the hypocrisy of his young wife and to the virtues of Lord Hardy, the son (by a first wife) whom he had disinherited. But the interest of the play is not in the plot. It is in the delightful fooling and flirtations of the coy Harriot and her impetuous Campley. It is in the exquisite bashfulness of the lovesick and tongue-tied Lady Sharlot and Lord Hardy :—

L. *Shar.* Now is the tender moment now approaching. (*aside*) There he is. (*They approach and salute each other Trembling.*) Your Lordship will please to sit ;

(*After a very long pause, stoln Glances, and irresolute Gesture.*)
Your Lordship I think has travell'd those parts of Italy
where the Armies Are—
Ld. *Har.* Yes Madam—
L. *Shar.* I think I have letters from You Dated
Mantua:
Ld. *Har.* I hope you have, Madam, and that their
purpose—
L. *Shar.* My Lord?— (*looking serious and confus'd.*)
Ld. *Har.* Was not your Ladiship going to say some-
thing?
L. *Shar.* I only attended to what your Lordship was
going to say—that is my Lord—But you were I be-
lieve going to say something of that Garden of the World
Italy—

And then there are the gaily satirical portraits of
Sable the undertaker and Puzzle the lawyer, and the
humours of Corporal Trim and his draggletailed recruits. The harangue with which Sable marshals his
mutes was quoted by Sydney Smith to illustrate his
definition of wit:—

You ungrateful Scoundrel, Did not I pity you, take you
out of a Great Man's Service, and show you the Pleasure
of receiving Wages? Did not I give you Ten, then
Fifteen, now Twenty shillings a Week, to be Sorrowful
and the more I give you, I think, the Glader you are?

And Trim's advice to his recruits, with its vivid suggestion of a lost London, is not less delightful in
another way :—

There's a thousand things you might do to help out
about this Town—as to cry—Puff—Puff Pyes—have
you any Knives or Syzzars to Grind—or, late in an Evening, whip from Grub-Street—strange and bloody News
from Flanders—Votes from the House of Commons—
Buns, rare Buns—Old Silver-Lace, Cloaks, Sutes or
Coats—Old Shoes, Boots or Hats.

Steele's sentimentality, for good and for bad, is already very much in evidence in *The Funeral.* We owe to it the charm and the freshness of the young lovers, and the ' pretty ' vivacity of Trim's wooing of his ' Dear Sempstress ' Mademoiselle d'Epingle. But it is responsible too for the unctuous figures of Trusty and Lord Brumpton. The former is a sentimentalist of the lachrymose type :—

> Forgive me my honour'd Master, (*Weeps, runs to my lord, and hugs him.*) I've often carry'd you in these Arms that Grasp you, they were stronger then, but if I Die to morrow, you're worth 5000*l.* by my Gift, 'tis what I've got in the Family, and I return it to you with thanks.

The latter is more inclined to sententious platitudes :—

> Ld. *B.* How dizzey a place is this World You live in !
> All Human Life's a mere Vertigo !
> *Tru.* Ay, ay, my lord, fine Reflections, fine Reflections.

But it is in the fifth act, when the reunion of Lord Brumpton and his son sends everybody off into blank verse, that the sentimentalism comes to a climax. It is difficult to take seriously, as the writing collapses in proportion as the emotions are intensified. This, for example, is how Lord Brumpton addresses Lord Hardy :—

> Be good my Son, and be a Worthy Lord :
> For when our Shineing Virtues bless Mankind,
> We Disappoint the lived Malecontents,
> Who long to call our Noble Order Useless,
> Our All's in Danger, Sir, nor shall you dally,
> Your Youth away with your fine Wives.
> No, in your Countries Cause you shall meet Death,
> While feeble we with minds resign'd do wait it.

If there is worse blank verse than this, I have yet to meet it.

The Lying Lover: or, the Ladies Friendship, the alliterative title of Steele's second comedy, is said to have been 'damn'd for its Piety'. It is, indeed, a distinctly solemn play. It appears to have been written in a deliberate attempt to conform with the dictates of Jeremy Collier. The liar is Bookwit, who 'makes false Love, gets drunk, and kills his Man; but in the fifth Act awakes from his Debauch, with the Compunction and Remorse which is suitable to a Man's finding Himself in a Gaol for the Death of his Friend, without knowing His why'. The soliloquy which Bookwit delivers in Newgate is almost too bad to be true :—

> We may feel Comfort by our Self-persuasion.
> But oh! there is no taking away Guilt!
> This divine Particle will ake for ever,
> There is no help but whence I dare not ask ;
> When this material Organ's indispos'd,
> Juleps can cool, and Anodines give rest,
> But nothing mix with this celestial Drop,
> But Dew from that high Heaven of which 'tis part.

Steele's own comment is that the 'Anguish He there expresses, and the mutual Sorrow between an only Child, and a tender Father in that Distress, are, perhaps, an Injury to the Rules of Comedy; but I am sure they are a Justice to those of Morality'. On the whole there is not very much more to be said for *The Lying Lover*. It is the minor characters who give the play what distinction it has. There is a romantic abigail called Lettice whom we discover deep in Sir Philip Sidney's *Arcadia*, 'reading by a small Candle. Two large ones by her unlighted.' There is Storm the highwayman and Charcoal the forger who welcome Bookwit into prison. And there is the footman Simon whose cry of 'Thieves! Thieves! Thieves!', as he is made to 'strip for Garnish' in Newgate, is the one irresistibly comic touch in the play. We should like to have seen more of them.

The Tender Husband is Steele's dramatic master-piece. It is unfortunate, therefore, that all the credit for it cannot be ascribed to him. An undefined share, consisting of 'many applauded Stroaks' and a pro-logue, was contributed by Addison, and the problem of where Steele ended and where Addison began is still unsolved. It is possible, as Forster suggested, that the character of Sir Harry Gubbin (a kind of prototype of the Tory Foxhunter in *The Freeholder*) may have been Addison's, and it is tempting, re-membering Leonora's library in *The Spectator*, with 'The Grand Cyrus: With a Pin stuck in one of the middle Leaves', to assign Biddy Tipkin to the same hand.

In spite of the dedication to Addison, in which Steele assures his friend that he has 'been very care-ful to avoid everything that might look Ill-natur'd, Immoral, or prejudicial to what the Better Part of Mankind hold Sacred and Honourable,' the didacti-cism and the sentimentality of *The Lying Lover* are conspicuous by their absence. The plot is as cynical and heartless as in a Restoration piece. It is the old theme of fortune-hunting. The hunters are Captain Clerimont (who captures the romantic, and wealthy, Biddy Tipkin) and Fainlove (the 'cast mistress' of Clerimont's brother), who entraps the gaping Hum-phrey Gubbin. It is characteristic that our sympathy is with the fortune-hunters all the time. The repre-sentatives of law and order, old Tipkin and that

' Weezel-fac'd cross old Gentleman with Spindle-Shanks ', Sir Harry Gubbin, only excite our contempt. The tone is set at the first appearance of Captain Clerimont and his friend Pounce. They are discussing the great Lombard Street heiress Miss Tipkin :—

Pou. To my knowledge Ten thousand Pounds in Money.

Ca. *Cl.* Such a Stature, such a Blooming Countenance, so easy a Shape !

Pou. In Jewels of her Grandmother's five thousand—

Ca. *Cl.* Her Wit so lively, her Mein so alluring !

Pou. In Land a Thousand a Year.

Ca. *Cl.* Her Lips have that certain Prominence, that Swelling softness, that they invite to a pressure; her Eyes that Languer, that they give Pain, tho' they look only inclin'd to rest—Her whole Person that one Charm— . . .

Pou. Why I thought you had never seen her—

Ca. *Cl.* No more I han't.

Pou. Who told you then of her inviting Lips, her soft sleepy Eyes—

Ca. *Cl.* You, yourself—

Pou. Sure you rave, I never spoke of her afore to you.

Ca. *Cl.* Why, you won't face me down—Did you not just now say, she had 10000*l.* in Money, five in Jewels, and a Thousand a Year ?

The wooing and winning of Miss Tipkin and the cajoling of Master Gubbin are conducted in the same spirit of engaging impudence. The ethics of the situation do not enter into the question at all. Everything is still in a state of nature and the quick wits of Clerimont and his accomplices prey upon the follies of their victims as irresistibly as a stoat upon a rabbit.

Humphry Gubbin has been compared often enough to Tony Lumpkin. The resemblance, indeed, is sufficiently striking.　They are both awkward, high-spirited country boobies; they have both been en-dowed with an infinite capacity for getting into mischief; and (a detail that seems to convict Gold-smith of plagiarism) they both boggle at marrying their cousins. Tony, however, who had only a doat-ing mother to get round, was the more happily cir-cumstanced.　Humphry's father, Sir Harry Gubbin, was made of sterner stuff than Mrs. Hardcastle. There is an admirable moment in which he disposes of his son's conscientious scruples :—

> *Hum.* But harke'e, Unkle, I have a Scruple I had better mention before Marriage than after.
>
> *Tip.* What's that.　What's that ?
>
> *Hum.* My Cousin, you know, is a Kin to me, and I don't think it Lawful for a young Man to Marry his own Relations.
>
> Sir *Ha.* Harke'e, harke'e, Numps : We have got a Way to solve all that, Sirrah! Consider this Cudgel! Your Cousin ! suppose I'd have you Marry your Grandmother! What then ?　　　　　　　　　　　　　　　　(*apart.*)
>
> *Tip.* Well, has your Father satisfy'd you in the Point, Mr. Humphry?
>
> *Hum.* Ay, ay, Sir, very well : I have not the least scruple remaining, No, no,—not in the least, Sir.

In any case, I am not sure that Tony would have surrendered so tamely.　There was more spirit and more ingenuity in him than in his surly, thick-headed prototype.

Biddy Tipkin, on the other hand, is descended from Molière's *précieuses ridicules* and is the ancestress of Lydia Languish. 'A perfect Quixot in Petticoats ', she passes the time with Philocles, Artaxerxes, Oroon-dates and the other princes of the French romances. It is her ambition to be another Elesmonda, Clidamira,

or Deidamia, but she has a serious obstacle to overcome in her very bourgeois name:—

> *Nei.* . . . if you ask my name, I must confess you put
> me upon Revealing what I always keep as the greatest
> Secret I have—for would you believe it—They have
> called me—I don't know how to own it, but they have
> called me—Bridget.
> *Capt.* Bridget?
> *Nei.* Bridget.
> *Capt.* Bridget?
> *Nei.* Spare my Confusion, I beseech you, Sir, and if
> you have occasion to mention me, let it be by Parthe-
> nissa, for that's the Name I have assum'd ever since
> I came to years of Discretion.

It is interesting to note that the acrimonious Dennis
attacked Biddy as an anachronism, arguing that ' if
a Comick Poet does not paint the Times in which he
lives, he does nothing at all ', and adding that ' the
reading of Romances and books of Knight-errantry '
had gone out of fashion years before. He was writing
in 1719, but the popularity of Mrs. Lenox's *The
Female Quixote* (which was published as late as 1752)
suggests that the vogue of the old romances was
a long time in dying.

The subsidiary plot, which gives the play its title,
is taken up with an intrigue between Fainlove (a
woman disguised as a fop) and Mrs. Clerimont, and
culminates in Mrs. Clerimont's surrender, their sur-
prisal by Clerimont—he is the Captain's brother—
and the humiliation of Mrs. Clerimont. It is un-
savoury in tone and makes unpleasant reading.

In the years after 1705 there is a gap in Steele's
dramatic activities. That his interest in the theatre
was still vigorous is proved by the dramatic criticism

in *The Tatler*, *The Spectator*, *Town-Talk*, *The Theatre*, and elsewhere, and in 1714 he became a sort of sleeping partner in the Drury Lane management. But marriages, business affairs, journalism, and politics occupied all his time. It was not until 1719 that he at last found time to begin the comedy, based upon Terence's *Andria*, which was first called *The Fine Gentleman*, later *The Unfashionable Lovers*, and finally *The Conscious Lovers*. The principal characters of the play made their first appearance in *The Theatre*, one of the last of Steele's numerous periodicals. Lucinda is described there as ' a young Woman of a most unaffected, easy and engaging Behaviour '; Charles Myrtle is a virtuous Templar with the single fault of jealousy ; Sealand is ' a true Pattern of that kind of third Gentry, which has arose in the World this last Century ' ; and Humphry is a faithful ' Valet de Chambre '.[1]   In a later number of *The Theatre* Steele, in the character of Sir John Edgar, added some further details :—

A Friend of Mine, who was lately preparing a Comedy according to the just Laws of the Stage, had formed a character of a Gentleman very patient of injuries where he did not think himself authorized to resent them, but equally impatient upon occasions wherein it is his duty to exert anger and resentment. The third Act of

[1] Humphrey cuts a more amusing figure here than he does in *The Conscious Lovers*.—' I cannot accuse him but of one ungentlemanly Thing, during our whole Time together ; and that was, He brought a Taylor to see me as I walk'd in Lincoln's Inn Garden, and sold him the Coat I then had on my Back, while I was musing concerning the Course of Human Affairs in the Upper Walk. This I cannot call an Injustice, for I had given him the Suit, and he put me in it, because it was warm, the Day after I gave it him being cold '.

this Comedy, which had not some accidents prevented, would have been performed before this Time, has a scene in it, wherein the first character bears unprovoked wrongs, denies a duel, and still appears a man of honour and courage.

The accident which is hinted at seems to have been the indifference of the other managers, who 'dozed over the perusal, and in the end unanimously condemned it'. Cibber, however, came to Steele's rescue and 'offered to enliven it with the characters of Tom and Phillis'. 'The spirit with which Colley executed his part', Derrick remarks, 'is well known; and for some of the most pleasant speeches in the play, we are indebted to his vast sense of humour.'

The plot is that of the *Andria*, and one or two of the scenes are actually translated from Terence. The Pamphilus is Bevil. His father, Sir John Bevil, intends to marry him to Lucinda, and Lucinda's father, Sealand, is also in favour of the match. But Mrs. Sealand wishes her daughter to marry a certain Cimberton, 'a Coxcomb', and Lucinda herself is in love with Myrtle, the Charinus of the *Andria*. A filial respect for his father, 'carried', in Dennis's opinion, 'a great deal too far', prevents Bevil declining the match, but his heart is with a mysterious Indiana, the Glycerium of Terence, an orphan whom he has brought from France and is maintaining, in the strictest respectability, in London. The difficulties in which every one is involved are finally solved by the discovery that Indiana is a long-lost daughter of Sealand's.[1]

---

[1] The plot is full of improbabilities. Dennis pointed out the unlikelihood of Sealand's wishing, or even being able, to retain his assumed name. All the substantial Bristol merchants were

The characterization is in the conventions of the sentimentalists. Sir John is the ideally affectionate father and Bevil the ideally affectionate son. Humphry, the representative of Terence's Sosia, is the faithful old family retainer. And Indiana is, in Hazlitt's words, 'as listless, and as insipid, as a drooping figure on an Indian screen'. It is a relief to turn to the two servants, Phillis and Tom. How far they are the creation of Cibber and how far they are Steele's is not clear, but one scene, and that the best in the play, is undoubtedly Steele's. It is that in which Tom recalls to Phillis the details of their first meeting, and it is based upon one of Steele's own papers in *The Guardian* :—

> *Tom.* It was on the first of April, one thousand seven hundred and fifteen, I came into Mr. Sealand's Service ; I was then a Hobble-de-Hoy, and you a pretty little tight Girl, a favourite Handmaid of the Housekeeper.— At that Time, we neither of us knew what was in us : I remember, I was order'd to get out of the window, one pair of Stairs, to rub the Sashes clean—the Person employ'd, on the inner side, was your charming self, whom I had never seen before.
>
> *Phil.* I think, I remember the silly Accident : What made ye, you Oaf, ready to fall down into the Street ?
>
> *Tom.* You know not, I warrant you—You could not guess what surpriz'd me. You took no Delight, when you immediately grew wanton, in your conquest, and put your Lips close, and breath'd upon the Glass, and

well known in London. He also showed that Bevil's silence to Indiana is unreasonable. He could have told her that he loved her, even if they were not able to marry until later. Dennis finally proved that Indiana could never have fallen into the hands of a Toulon privateer on a voyage to India, and that once arrived at Toulon she must immediately have communicated with her English friends. The objections are distinctly interesting.

when my Lips approach'd, a dirty Cloth you rubb'd
against my Face, and hid your beauteous Form ; when
I again drew near, you spit, and rubb'd, and smil'd
at my Undoing.

Phil. What silly Thoughts you Men have !

' We are here once more ', Hazlitt exclaimed on reading this scene, ' in the company of our old friend,
Isaac Bickerstaff, Esq.'

iii

Steele has never been ranked very high as a dramatist, even by his apologists. It is probable, indeed,
that his plays are rather better than it has been
customary to admit. I would not hesitate to put him
on a level with Dekker or Shirley or, to come down
to our own times, with Sir James Barrie. His
comedies are alive ; they have what the cant of
criticism used to call *vivida vis.* It is true his deficiencies are serious and glaring. Apparently a
feeling for construction was totally lacking in
Steele. His substitute for it was a lavish ingenuity
in elaborating intricacies of plot, of most of which
he is never able to make use. A typical example
occurs in *The Conscious Lovers,* though that play
(perhaps because of Cibber's assistance) is on the
whole the least unsatisfactory in this respect. The
misanthropy of Indiana's aunt was due to ' the Behaviour of one Man to myself'. Who was this man ?
It is possible that Sealand is meant, but a false lover
certainly seems to be indicated. The mystery is
never cleared up or referred to again. Analogous to
this is Steele's habit of introducing characters which
impede instead of advancing the progression of the
play. Sable and Puzzle and Trim's recruits in *The*

Funeral, Storm and Charcoal in *The Lying Lover*, are cases in point. They are all, in the strict sense, irrelevant; that they provide some of the most attractive scenes in these plays is only additional evidence of the perversity of Steele's dramatic instincts.

The occasional uncertainty, cumbrousness, and obscurity of the dialogue are more remarkable. They might be attributed to carelessness or hurry, were they not particularly evident in the most ambitious scenes. An example is the celebrated duel scene in *The Conscious Lovers*. In the preface to that play we are informed that 'the whole was writ for the sake of the Scene of the Fourth Act, wherein Mr. Bevill evades the Quarrel with his Friend'; but it is precisely in this scene that the cumbrousness of the dialogue is most obvious. The climax of the scene is Bevil's soliloquy:—

> Shall I (though provok'd to the Uttermost) recover myself at the Entrance of a third Person, and that my Servant too, and not have Respect enough to all I have ever been receiving from Infancy, the Obligation to the best of Fathers, to an unhappy Virgin too, whose Life depends on mine. (*Shutting the door.*) (*To* Myrtle.) I have, thank Heaven, had time to recollect my self, and shall not, for fear of what such a rash Man as you think of me, keep longer unexplain'd the false Appearances, under which your Infirmity of Temper makes you suffer; when, perhaps, too much Regard to a false Point of Honour, makes me prolong that Suffering.

What is one to make of it? Dennis characterized the English in this scene as 'awkward, clumsy, and spiritless'. It is, indeed, only a degree better than the blank verse which disfigures *The Funeral* and *The Lying Lover*.

The moral and sentimental preoccupations of Steele do not require to be emphasized. It is not unjust to describe them as sincere, but superficial and uninstructed. Hazlitt, who seems to have had something of a prejudice against Steele's plays, is not really unfair in this connexion. 'The author', he complains, ' seems to be all the time on his good behaviour, as if writing a comedy was no very creditable employment, and as if the ultimate object of his ambition was a dedication to the queen. Nothing can be better meant, or more inefficient. It is almost a misnomer to call them comedies; they are rather homilies in dialogue, in which a number of very pretty ladies and gentlemen discuss the fashionable topics of gaming, of duelling, of seduction, of scandal, &c., with a sickly sensibility, that shows as little hearty aversion to vice as sincere attachment to virtue.'

What are we to set against these defects? A certain freshness and naturalness in the characterization, particularly in his young girls, his Biddy and Sharlot and Harriot and Phillis. A good-tempered, good-natured sense of humour. ' Just strokes of Humour ', an admiring contemporary wrote,

> Just strokes of Humour St—le can best impart,
> And picture human Life with truest Art.

And finally an eye, the essayist's eye, for detail and colour. Perhaps if there had not been a *Tatler* or a *Spectator* we should not stop at this vignette of the New Exchange in *The Lying Lover* :—

> One little lisping Rogue, Ribbandths, Gloveths, Tippeths.—Sir, cries another, will you buy a fine Swordknot; then a third, pretty Voice and Curtsie ;—Does not your Lady want Hoods, Scarfs, fine green Silk

Stockings.—I went by as if I had been in Seraglio, a
living Gallery of Beauties,—staring from side to side, I
bowing, they laughing.

Or, in *The Funeral,* at Lady Brumpton's anticipations
of a visit to the theatre : —

What Pleasure 'twill be when my Lady Brumpton's Footman's call'd (who kept a place for that very purpose) to
make a suddain Insurrection of Fine Wigs in the Pit,
and Side-Boxes.   Then with a pretty sorrow in one's
Face, and a willing Blush for being Star'd at, one ven-
tures to look round and Bow, to one of one's own
Quality.   Thus (*very Derectly*) to a Smug Pretending
Fellow of no Fortune : Thus (*as scarce seeing him*) to
one that Writes Lampoons : Thus (*Fearfully*) to one one
really Loves : Thus (*looking down*) to one's Woman
Acquaintance, from Box to Box : Thus (*with looks
differently Familiar*).

Or at Sir Harry Gubbin's inventory of the furniture
in his brother's bedroom :—

A Suit of Tapestry Hangings, with the Story of Judith
and Holofernes, torn only where the Head should have
been off—an old Bedsted curiously wrought about the
Posts, consisting of two Load of Timber.   A Hoan,
a Basin, three Razors and a Comb-Case.

Or at Bookwit's little lyric upon the *belles* of the Mall
in November :—

Oh ! to see the dear things trip, trip along, and breath
so short, nipt with the Season.

As it is we prize most the passages in Steele's comedies
which recall us to his essays.   He was an essayist first
of all, a dramatist only secondarily.

IV

MRS CENTLIVRE

i

'WHAT a Pox have the Women to do with the Muses?' exclaims the Critick of *A Comparison between the Two Stages*. 'I hate these Petticoat Authors; 'tis false Grammar, there's no Feminine for the Latin word, 'tis entirely of the Masculine Gender, and the Language won't bear such a thing as a She-Author.' The tirade typifies the attitude of the world of culture in the face of the invasion of literature by the 'fair sex' which had begun with the Restoration. An authoress was still a monstrosity. It was not only ridiculous, it was against the nature of things for a woman to write. The prejudice was, no doubt, a simple matter of sex antagonism. It may, however, have received some support in the characters and records of the few professional authoresses the period possessed. Aphra Behn, Mrs. Manley, Elizabeth Thomas, and Eliza Haywood could not boast of very savoury careers. They were the best possible argument against a 'Petticoat-Author'.

> The modest Muse a Veil with Pity throws
> O'er Vice's Friends and Virtue's Female Foes;
> Abash'd she views the bold unblushing Mien
> Of modern Manley, Centlivre, and Behn.

Susanna Centlivre, the once 'celebrated Mrs. Centlivre', was no better and no worse than the others.

In her younger days she appears to have been something of an adventuress. 'She was inclined to be
very gay', is the reluctant admission of a feminine
admirer, and Boyer, another admirer, refers discreetly
to 'several gay Adventures (over which we shall
draw a Veil)'. It has been asserted that she was at
one time the mistress of the poet Anthony Hammond
and that she lived with him, when he was still an
undergraduate at Cambridge, in boy's clothes. She was
later 'married or something like it' to a Mr. Fox,
then to a Mr. Carrol (who was killed in a duel), and
finally and indisputably in 1706 to Joseph Centlivre,
a Huguenot refugee who became Queen Anne's cook.
A number of dates between 1667 and 1680 have been
proposed for the year of her birth, and she has been
provided with two fathers. It is certain that she died
in London on the 1st of December 1723.

In spite of a somewhat disreputable youth we are
told that Mrs. Centlivre later 'lived in a decent clean
Manner, and could show (which I believe few other
Poets could, who depended chiefly on their pen)
a great many Jewels and Pieces of Plate, which were
the Produce of her own Labour, either purchased by
the Money brought in by her copies, her Benefit-
Plays, or were Presents from Patrons'; and her
acquaintances included 'a great Number of Gentlemen of Eminence and Wit, particularly, Sir Richard
Steele, Mr. Rowe, Mr. Budgell, Dr. Sewel, Mr.
Amhurst, &c.' It is to be noted that these 'Gentlemen of Eminence and Wit' were all Whigs. Mrs.
Centlivre was an enthusiastic Whig herself, and this
was probably the origin of these connexions. Like
most of the Whig writers of the time she occupies
a niche in *The Dunciad*:—

At last Centlivre felt her voice to fail;
Motteux himself unfinish'd left his tale;
Boyer the State and Law the Stage gave o'er;
Morgan and Mandevil could prate no more.

Pope also attacked her in two pamphlets, *Revenge by Poison on the Body of Mr. Edmund Curll* and its sequel, *The most deplorable condition of Mr. Edmund Curll*, and it has recently been suggested by Mr. George Sherburn (mistakenly, I think) that she may have been the original of Phoebe Clinket in *Three Hours after Marriage*. The ostensible origin of these attacks was 'a Ballad against Mr. Pope's Homer before he began it', called *The Catholick Poet; or, Protestant Barnaby's Sorrowful Lamentation*, of which Pope suspected Mrs. Centlivre. It is a scurrilous poem, but there is evidence that Pope was wrong in attributing it to her.

ii

Mrs. Centlivre's nineteen plays include fourteen comedies, three farces, a tragedy, and a tragi-comedy, and range in date from 1700 to 1722. The farces, the tragedy, and the tragi-comedy, though the last has some amusing comic scenes, are almost completely worthless. It is upon the comedies, and not upon all of them by any means, that her reputation must rest. *The Beau's Duel*, *The Stolen Heiress*, *Love's Contrivance*, *The Platonick Lady*, *Mar-Plot*, *The Man's bewitch'd*, *The Perplex'd Lovers*, and *The Artifice*, may be mentioned only to be dismissed. *The Stolen Heiress* is a slovenly adaptation of a Caroline romantic comedy; *Love's Contrivance* is run together from two of Molière's farces; *The Man's bewitch'd* is a translation from the French dramatist Haute-

roche; and *The Perplex'd Lovers* is admittedly only
an English version of an unnamed Spanish play.
The Beau's Duel, The Platonick Lady, Mar-Plot, and
The Artifice are more or less original, but that is
the only claim to consideration they possess. With
the six comedies which remain—*The Gamester,
The Basset-Table, Love at a Venture, The Busie
Body, The Warder, A Bold Stroke for a Wife*—
the position is different. They have all a certain
vitality and technical *finesse*, and are as good examples
as one can hope to find of the work of the professional
dramatist of the eighteenth century. They have, it
must be admitted, no intellectual or literary signi-
ficance; the writing is never distinguished and the
characterization, with the single exception of Marplot
in *The Busie Body*, is conventional and superficial.
But the purpose for which they were written is ful-
filled, to a greater or less extent, in all of them.
They amuse, they distract the mind. Mrs. Centlivre's comedies occupy the position in the literature
of the eighteenth century that is now filled by a de-
tective story. They are the railway reading of
Georgian England.

The first of Mrs. Centlivre's plays to create something of a sensation was *The Gamester*. It is an
experiment in the Cibberian manner with an abun-
dance of ethical and sentimental motives, and as such
is only moderately successful. The theme, however,
is a picturesque one, and the local colour, with all the
technicalities of the gaming tables, is worked up well.
We hear the croupier calling the score. 'Seven's the
Main', 'Four to Seven', 'Four Trae-Ace', 'Duce,
Ace', 'Quator Duce', 'Cinque Duce'. We see the

unsuccessful gambler 'with Arms a cross, down cast Eyes, no Powder in his Perriwig; a Steenkirk tuck'd in to hide the Dirt, Sword-knot unty'd; no Gloves, and Hands and Face as dirty as a Tinker'. We are introduced to the 'back-hand tip', and the 'Doctors' or false dice. We hear the box-keeper warning the players not to 'stay late for fear of the Press-masters, here was two Gangs last night before twelve a Clock'.

The gamester of the title is the younger Valere, who hesitates between his darling vice and the charms of Angelica, who will not marry him until he has abjured gambling. The climax comes when Angelica, disguised as a young beau, wins a portrait of herself, which she had recently given Valere and which he had promised never to part with. Finally, of course, Valere repents and reforms his ways, and Angelica forgives and marries him. The bulk of the play is based upon Regnard's *Le Joueur*, but the sentimental conclusion is Mrs. Centlivre's own invention. In the French version Valère, after losing his beloved by staking her gift at the tables, remains to the end the slave of his ruling passion, consoling himself with the hope that

quelque jour
Le jeu m'acquittera des pertes de l'amour.

The difference is a piquant illustration of the contrasting ideals of the classical comedy of Regnard and the sentimental comedy of Mrs. Centlivre.

The Basset-Table was written as a pendant to *The Gamester*, the gambler in this case being a woman and the reformer a man. The connexion between the two plays is similar to that between *The Careless Husband* and *The Lady's Last Stake* of Cibber.

The hero and heroine are the virtuous Lord Worthy and the frivolous Lady Reveller, and their passages of arms are in the typically sentimental manner. In most of the scenes, however, the sentimentalism is obscured by the introduction of a number of the conventional types of Restoration Comedy. There is a Sir James Courtly, 'an airy Gentleman'; a Sir Richard Plainman, 'a great Lover of a Soldier, and an inveterate enemy to the French'; a bluff Captain Hearty; a Buckle and Alpiew, the pert footman and the perter waiting woman; and a Mr. and Mrs. Sago, a city couple who call each other 'Puddy' and 'Keecky' and indeed conduct all their conversation in a kind of baby language. The most original character is Valeria, who is described as a 'Philosophical Girl'. She comes in running—'don't stop me, I shall lose the first Insect for Desection, a huge Flesh Fly'. A little later she is discovered in her study, 'with Books upon a Table, a Microscope, putting Fish upon it, several Animals lying by'. She is a great reader of 'Discartes' and the other philosophers, and is confident that 'Custom would bring them as much in Fashion as Furbeloes'. Her curiosity is indefatigable, and the moment she is introduced to Captain Hearty she begins to inquire 'if ever you had the curiosity to inspect a Mermaid—Or if you are convinced there is a World in every Star'. It is disconcerting to find that she has a lover, but their billing and cooing usually resolves itself into a discussion of the 'Lumbricus Latus' and the 'Lumbricus teres Intestinalis' and similar mysteries. Alternatively they fish for eels in vinegar. To the modern reader Valeria is a rather pathetic figure. She means no harm, and she is not by any means a fool. It is true she is a blue-stocking, that is her only crime; but the eighteenth century was curiously merciless to blue-stockings.[1]

The Basset-Table, though it was less successful, is a rather better comedy than *The Gamester*. Perhaps it is because the tone is more consistently that of a comedy of manners, less realistic; perhaps because the moralizing and the sentimental issues, never quite sincere with Mrs. Centlivre, are not so emphasized. The dialogue is written with spirit and an, 'atmosphere' is maintained with considerable skill. The opening scene is probably the most effective. It is four o'clock in the morning, and the footmen and porters ('with Chairs, Torches, and Flambeaux') are sleepily waiting for the gambling party to break up. At last the basset comes to an end. The servants are to be heard shouting within. 'Mr. Looseall's Man', 'Mr. Sonica's Servant', 'Ha, Hy, my Lady Gamewel's Chair ready there'. 'Where the Devil', cries one footman, 'is my Flambeaux?' The porter tells another, 'your Lady has gone half an hour ago'. 'The Devil she is', he grumbles, 'why did you not call me?' The shouting begins again. 'My Lady Umbray's Coach there.' 'Hey! Will, pull up there.'

Love at a Venture, Mrs. Centlivre's third important play, was acted in the New Theatre at Bath, probably in 1706, by a travelling troupe acting under the patronage of the Duke of Grafton. Mrs. Centlivre is said to have taken one of the parts herself. In *The Laureat*, a not very trustworthy authority, it is stated that Mrs. Centlivre had offered the play to

---

[1] It has been suggested that Valeria was intended to caricature a contemporary feminist, Mary Astell, who is also satirized in *The Tatler*.

Cibber at Drury Lane. Cibber, however, though he
was later to appropriate many of its scenes for his
own *The Double Gallant*, refused it with scorn.
' Why, Madam, said he, ' This would be putting upon
the Audience indeed . . . 'tis extravagant, it is out-
raging Nature, it is silly, and it is not ridiculous.'
If the episode is not fictitious, Cibber certainly made
a mistake. *Love at a Venture* is a very pleasant
comedy, at least as good and probably better than
Thomas Corneille's *Le Galand Doublé*, upon which it
is based. *The Gamester* and *The Basset-Table*, though
primarily experiments in the fashionable sentimentalism, had shown that Mrs. Centlivre's real talent
lay rather in a lively reproduction of the manners
and atmosphere of contemporary society. The sentiment was false, but the animation was genuine and
unquestionable. *Love at a Venture* is an advance upon
the earlier plays because it has discarded sentiment
altogether. It is definitely more in the Restoration
mode than the majority of Mrs. Centlivre's comedies.
The licence of Bellair, ' A Gentleman just come from
Travel; an Airy Spark '; the snivelling senility of
Sir Paul Cautious; the vapid fatuity of Wou'dbe—they
are all more typical of the Restoration than of Queen
Anne. And the dialogue, particularly that of Bellair
and his friend Sir William, has a sparkle which was
becoming rarer every year. An additional interest
is the skill with which the intrigue is conducted.
There is an admirable scene in which Bellair appears
before Camilla and Beliza, at one moment as a Colonel
Revell, the lover of Beliza and a man of the world just
back from Portugal, at the next as a Mr. Constant,
Camilla's lover and a steady-going country squire
' come up about a Law-Suit ', and with such assurance

and ingenuity that he ends by convincing them. The theme, Bellair's promiscuity in amour, is naturally sometimes a little audacious; but it is never gross, and the final impression the comedy leaves is one of gaiety, the gaiety of the inimitable and (in spite of his outrageous behaviour) very likeable Bellair.

Love at a Venture was the first of Mrs. Centlivre's plays to exhibit to the full her ingenuity in the manipulation of intrigue. In this it was an interesting forerunner of her masterpiece, indeed the only one of her comedies which is still almost readable, *The Busie Body*. It has been called the most remarkable comedy of intrigue in English, and its supremacy in this respect was recognized by Steele on its first appearance. 'The Plot', he wrote in a short notice in *The Tatler*, 'and Incidents of the Play are laid with that Subtilty of Spirit which is peculiar to Females of Wit, and is very seldom well performed by those of the other Sex, in whom Craft in Love is an Act of Invention, and not as with Women, the Effect of Nature and Instinct.' Unfortunately the best comedy of intrigue is apt to lose its savour when it comes down from the stage. The brilliance of its surprises and the excitement of its coincidences tend to evaporate on the printed page. A sympathetic imagination, quick to respond to the effectiveness of a situation in the theatre and willing to overlook occasional crudities and improbabilities of detail, is required for a thorough appreciation of *The Busie Body*. It is a play which demands the co-operation of the actor and the painted scene, and in their absence it may easily fall a little flat.

Two more or less parallel plots make up the play.

Sir George Airy is in love with Miranda, but is at the
mercy of her avaricious guardian, Sir Francis Gripe,
who wishes to marry her himself.   Sir Francis's son
Charles and Isabinda are also in love, but Isabinda's
father refuses to allow them to meet.   There are
plots and counterplots of considerable ingenuity.   In
the end both of the loving couples are successful, but
their success throughout is always all but prevented
by the well-intended but unlucky interferences of
the busybody of the title, the unfortunate Marplot,
another of Sir Francis's wards.   Marplot is the real,
if the unconscious, hero of *The Busie Body*.   Hazlitt,
in his telling way, has called him 'a standing
memorial of unmeaning vivacity and assiduous impertinence'.   He is one of the most attractive of
literature's simpletons, a stepbrother, if not of Slen-
der or Sir Andrew Aguecheek, at least of the gulls
and ninnies, the Stephens and Fitzdottrels, of Ben
Jonson's plays.   Mrs. Centlivre has characterized
him in the list of the *dramatis personae* as ' A sort
of a silly Fellow, Cowardly, but very Inquisitive to
know every Body's Business, generally spoils all
he undertakes, yet without Design'; but that is both
an understatement and unfair.   It is true Marplot
is not fond of fighting, but that is 'purely to be
serviceable to my Friends'.   There is no limit
to his good-nature.   Even the ungrateful Charles
finds 'a thousand Conveniences in him, he'll lend me
his Money when he has any, run of my Errands and
be proud on't; in short, he'll Pimp for me, Lye for
me, Drink for me, do anything but Fight for me'.
He has his little weaknesses.   He is something of
a snob and would give ten guineas to be introduced
to 'a Man of Wit'.   'Well', he reflects in his inno-

cence, ''tis a vast Addition to a Man's Fortune,
according to the Rout of the World, to be seen in the
Company of Leading Men', and he assures Sir George
that 'a Bow from the side Box or to be seen in your
Chariot, binds me ever yours'. But his ruling passion
is not snobbery but inquisitiveness. 'Business, and
I not know it, Egad, I'll watch him,' 'why the
Devil should not one know every Man's Concern?'
'I shall go stark Mad, if I'm not let into this Secret'
—his curiosity is always wringing from him exclama-
tions of this sort. 'Lord, lord,' he sighs (the reflection has a Pepysian ring), 'How little Curiosity some
People have! Now my chief pleasure lies in knowing
every body's Business.' It is a demon which possesses
him, and the itch of his curiosity makes him the
burden of his friends, while the goodness of his heart,
reinforced by the weakness of his head, is always
delivering him into the hands of their enemies. He
is involved in a perpetual whirl of abuse and castiga-
tion, and the last we hear of him he is pitying himself,
still blissfully unaware that he has only himself to
thank for his misfortunes. 'So here's every body
happy, I find, but poor Pilgarlick. I wonder what
Satisfaction I shall have for being cuff'd, kick'd, and
beaten in your Service.' Dryden's Sir Martin Marall
must have been the model for Marplot. But Marplot
is not by any means a mere copy. He wears his
folly with a difference. He is absurd, but he is never,
like Sir Martin, contemptible. He is, after all, a gentleman, and he is not altogether a nincompoop; even
Charles has to admit that 'The Dog is diverting
sometimes, or there wou'd be no enduring his Impertinence'. Sir Martin was never anything more
than a walking vacancy.

The Wonder: A Woman keeps a Secret and *A Bold Stroke for a Wife* are two comedies which are often set by the side of *The Busie Bodie.* They belong to the same *genus* certainly, that of the comedy of intrigue. They exhibit similarly ingenious situations; they are bristling with parallel complications and misunderstandings. But they are *The Busie Body* without Marplot. Their characterization is conventional and superficial (Don Felix in *The Wonder* is a partial exception) and it is difficult, in the absence of the actors, to take much interest in the fortunes and misfortunes of such obvious puppets. The problems which beset the lovers in these plays become, in the reading, almost algebraic. Let *a* represent the heavy father, let *b* be the comic servant, let *c* be the passionate *jeune premier.* We can imagine Mrs. Centlivre working it out like a sum on the blackboard. There is no doubt, however, that the acting made all the difference. For one thing, *The Wonder* (with Wilks or Garrick in the role of Don Felix) was one of the most popular plays of the century. For another, Hazlitt, who could still see these plays at Covent Garden and Drury Lane, has praised *The Wonder* with an infectious enthusiasm the sincerity of which it is impossible to question. The passage is in the *Lectures on the English Comic Writers* and is too good not to be quoted.

'The "Wonder" is one of the best of our acting plays. The passion of jealousy in Don Felix is managed in such a way as to give as little offence as possible to the audience, for every appearance combines to excite and confirm his worst suspicions, while we, who are in the secret, laugh at his groundless uneasiness and apprehensions. The ambiguity of the heroine's situation, which is like a continued practical *equivoque*, gives rise to a quick succession of causeless alarms, subtle excuses, and the most hairbreadth 'scapes. The scene near the end, in which Don Felix, pretending to be drunk, forces his way out of Don Manuel's house, who wants to keep him a prisoner, by producing his marriage-contract in the shape of a pocket-pistol, with the terrors and confusion into which the old gentleman is thrown by this sort of *argumentum ad hominem*, is one of the richest treats the stage affords, and calls forth incessant peals of laughter and applause. Besides the two principal characters (Violante and Don Felix), Lissardo and Flippanta come in very well to carry on the underplot; and the airs and graces of an amorous waiting-maid and conceited man-servant, each copying after their master and mistress, were never hit off with more natural volubility or affected *nonchalance* than in this enviable couple. Lissardo's playing off the diamond ring before the eyes of his mortified Dulcinea, and aping his master's absent manner while repeating—" Roast me these Violantes ", as well as the jealous quarrel of two waiting-maids, which threatens to end in some very extraordinary discoveries, are among the most amusing traits in this comedy. Colonel Briton, the lover of Clara, is a spirited and enterprising soldier of fortune; and his servant Gibby's undaunted, incorrigible blundering, with a dash of nationality in it, tells in a very edifying way.'

Although Hazlitt has omitted *A Bold Stroke for a Wife* from his survey, the case is much the same with it as with *The Wonder*. There can be no doubt that a play which has contributed to the language the

once proverbial expression 'the real Simon Pure'
must have been a popular favourite.   But it is difficult now to recapture the first rapture of our ancestors.
A Bold Stroke for a Wife is not absolutely unreadable,
but it cannot be called a good play.   It is, however,
better written than *The Wonder* and the plot is easier to
follow.   The centre of all the intrigues is Mrs. Lovely.
She has been provided by her father with four guardians.   They are Sir Philip Modelove, ' an old Beau,
that has May in his Fancy and Dress, but December
in his Face and his Heels ; he admires nothing but
new Fashions, and those must be French ; loves
Operas, Balls, Masquerades, and is always the most
tawdry of the whole Company on a Birth-day ';
Periwinkle, ' a kind of Virtuoso, a silly, half-witted
Fellow, but positive and surly ; fond of nothing but
what is Antique and Foreign, and wears his Cloaths
of the Fashion of the last Century ; doats upon Tra-
vellers, and believes Sir John Mandiville more than
the Bible ' ; Tradelove, a merchant, ' a Fellow that
will out-lie the Devil for the Advantage of Stock, and
cheat his father that got him in a Bargain ' ; and
Obadiah Prim, a Quaker.   The play is taken up with
the various devices and disguises by which Colonel
Fainwell, having already secured the affections of
Mrs. Lovely herself, tricks the guardians, one by one,
into consenting to the marriage.   The interest of the
piece is to a certain extent in the ' humours ' of the
guardians, but for the most part it consists in the con-
stantly renewed, but somewhat mechanical, ingenuity
of the intrigue.

iii

Mrs. Centlivre, quite rightly, has not fared well at the hands of the critics. She was sneered at by Cibber and by Pope; she was patronized by the *Biographia Dramatica*; and more recently Mr. G. H. Nettleton has shaken a professorial head over the indecency of her plays. The only critics who have written of Mrs. Centlivre with some enthusiasm are Hazlitt and, rather surprisingly, A. W. Ward—and even Ward concludes his appreciation with the admission that 'in style and in the contrivance of situations she habitually sinks to the lowest level of our post-Restoration drama, exhibiting no trace of sympathy with the better and purer tone which was gradually gaining ground in English comedy'. Hazlitt, on the other hand, professed to discern in her plays 'a provoking spirit and a volatile salt' which 'still preserves them from decay'. He praised her 'intricate involution and artful *dénouement* of the plot'. He applauded 'the archness of the humour and sly allusion to the most delicate points'.

The indecency at which Hazlitt hints and to which Professor Nettleton objects must be conceded. It is even objectionably present in the tragi-comedy of *The Perjur'd Husband*. But elsewhere it is of no importance; it is scarcely ever offensive or embarrassing, never merely gross. Indeed, in comparison with her predecessors and with many of her contemporaries Mrs. Centlivre is almost spotless. The suspicion of immodesty which remains, the vague aroma of *doubles entendres*, are far from objectionable. They impart a flavour to the plays; they are the spices in the comic soup.

Mrs. Centlivre was a professional dramatist, and her plays are specifically acting plays. Their effectiveness is one of action and of *ensemble*, not of detail. They are without the brilliance of dialogue and the sparkle of antithesis which a reading play possesses. Their language is sometimes, as the *Biographia Dramatica* complained, 'poor, enervate, incorrect and puerile'. It is almost always careless, abrupt, and without distinction. Like Dryden's Og, Mrs. Centlivre could 'doe anything but write'. But she had vivacity, vitality, and ingenuity. The characters in her comedies, though perhaps not one is original, are always to a greater or less extent animated. A few of them, Marplot certainly and perhaps Don Felix, are really alive. She was particularly successful in the depiction of impudence. The impertinence of her fine gentlemen is only excelled by that of their servants. Valere has no rival except Hector, or Britton except Gibby. And it is as much the impudent curiosity as the inanity of Marplot which appeals to us, just as it is the brazenness rather than the ingenuity of Bellair which is so attractive.

Hazlitt, writing of a performance of *The Wonder* at Covent Garden in 1816, speaks of it as a 'brilliant series of mis-timed exits and entrances'. It is an admirable definition of that quality in which Mrs. Centlivre is supreme. It is a genius for dove-tailing one laughable incident into another, for begetting ludicrous mistake upon ludicrous mistake. Mrs. Centlivre has no equal in the talent—though it may not be always appreciated in the reading—of disposing her *dramatis personae* into convenient closets and discovering them at inconvenient moments. She is without a rival in the possibilities she can detect in disguises, and in mistakes of identity. Indeed, to modern eyes, it often degenerates into a reckless defiance of realism. But within the conventions of her theatre she is a master-mechanic of dramatic construction. The prologue to *The Artifice* has put her merits not unfairly:—

> Ask not, in such a General Dearth, much Wit,
> If she your Taste in Plot, and Humor hit :
> Plot, Humor, Business, form the Comic Feast,
> Wit's but a higher-relish'd Sauce at best ;
> And when too much, like Spice, destroys the Taste.

It is Mrs. Centlivre's justification that she did hit this taste, and her reward was that her comedies kept the stage much longer than many inherently better plays. They were popular throughout the eighteenth century, and *The Busie Body* and *The Wonder* survived well into the nineteenth. Etherege by that time was forgotten and Wycherley had beeen carefully 'doctored' into respectability, but Lamb and Hazlitt were able to laugh as heartily over the 'broad shining face, the orbicular rolling of his eye, and the alarming drop of his chin' of Munden as Marplot as their great-grandfathers may have done at the antics of Pack in the same part.

V

JOHN GAY

i

'**A** LITTLE, round, French abbé of a man, sleek, soft-hearted', Gay is the most immediately likeable of the wits of the Scriblerus Club. The world is still a little afraid of Swift, the terrible Dean with the flashing blue eyes, 'quite azure as the heavens'; Arbuthnot, Atterbury, and the others are only half remembered; and Pope—well, it is certainly easier to respect than to like Pope. It was not very different in the eighteenth century. Voltaire, who had known the whole circle in his younger days, once told an English traveller who had found his way to Ferney that 'he admired Swift and loved Gay vastly'. That is what we all feel. The laughing round face which looks out of Kneller's sketch in the National Portrait Gallery is as open and as irresistible as a boy's. 'Gay was quite a natural man,' Pope told Spence, 'wholly without art or design, and spoke just what he thought and as he thought it'. It was this naturalness which was the secret of the attraction he exercised upon his reserved and sophisticated contemporaries. In a world of cynics Gay was a portent, a prodigy like the ingenuous Huron in Voltaire's novel.

> Of Manners gentle, of Affections mild,
> In Wit, a Man; Simplicity a Child.

The often quoted lines have been ponderously trounced by Dr. Johnson, but there is more of Gay in them, if there is less of poetry, than in the devil-may-care epicureanism of the epitaph Gay wrote for himself :—

> Life is a jest; and all things show it,
> I thought so once; but now I know it.

His epicureanism was not Byronic and picturesque ; it was more placid and sensual, the philosophy of a red-faced country squire.

A certain idiosyncrasy and charm distinguished Gay as a companion, and there are the same qualities in his writings. *Trivia: or, the Art of Walking the Streets of London*, with its detailed portraits of the link boys and the chairmen, the sweeps, the small coal-men, the milkmaids, and the Mohocks of the eighteenth-century London, is as perennially fresh as the rainbow ; and *The Shepherd's Week*, for all that it was primarily a parody of Namby-Pamby Philips, is nearer Theocritus than any other pastoral in English. We would rather go maying with his Bowzybeus or the uncouth Blouzelinda,

> Set off with kerchief starch'd and pinners clean,

than with the most bedizened of Pope's nymphs and shepherds. We would not exchange Molly Mog or black-eyed Susan for Belinda herself. 'Charm', an individual and indefinable magic, was Gay's distinguishing characteristic, and it has been for this 'charm', rather than for any more solid qualities, that the twentieth century has been flocking out to his plays at Mr. Playfair's theatre in Hammersmith.

ii

It was not until January 1728 that *The Beggar's Opera* made Gay very rich and Rich very gay. But the 'Newgate pastoral' was not by any means the

first piece the poet had written for the theatres. It
was not even his first play to make a 'hit' with the
town. Two farces, two comedies, a tragedy, and a
pastoral had preceded *The Beggar's Opera*; and at
least two of these, *The What D'Ye Call It* and *Three
Hours after Marriage*, had scored a decided success.
The Beggar's Opera was also followed by two ballad
operas, a comedy, and a farce. It was not a solitary
prodigy, but the culmination of a dramatic career
which had been a series of similar experiments and
innovations.

The Mohocks, A Tragi-Comical Farce was the first
of Gay's experiments with the drama. It is partly a
topical satire, an exposure not so much of the Mohocks
themselves—the rowdy young bloods we have with
us always—as of the consternation and dismay which
they inspired. It is partly a farce, the crude but
always laughable farce of inappropriate physical
terrors. And it is partly a burlesque. Abaddon, the
Emperor, discourses to his subjects in blank verse
perhaps parodying Dryden's :—

> Thus far our Riots with Success are crown'd,
> Have found no stop, or what they found o'ercame ;
> In vain th' embattell'd Watch in deep array,
> Against our Rage oppose their lifted Poles ;
> Through Poles we rush triumphant, Watchman rolls
> On Watchman ;

and the oaths that Gogmagog imposes subsequently
are an obvious parody of *Hamlet*. The embattled
watch, on the other hand, worthy successors of Dog-
berry and Verges, do not rise above prose :—

> They make no more of our Poles than so many Straws ;
> let me tell you, Sir, that I have seen them do such

things that would make a Man's Hair stand on end—
let me see—ay—to-morrow Night, 'twill be three Nights
ago—when I was going my round—I met about five or
six and thirty of these Mohocks—by the same token 'twas
a very windy Morning—they all had Swords as broad as
Butchers Cleavers, and hack'd and hew'd down all before
them—I saw—as I am a Man of credit, in the Neigh-
bourhood—all the Ground covered with Noses—as thick
as 'tis with Hail-stones after a Storm.

In the battle of the watch-house which ensues, the
watchmen are ignominiously defeated and compelled
to change clothes with the Mohocks, who march
them off to the Justices to be punished for their
captors' offences. It is only at the very last moment
that the truth comes out and the tables are turned and
the Mohocks taken off to prison.

The novelty of *The Mohocks* was its fusion of the
three *genres*, hitherto unconnected in the drama, of
topical satire, farce, and burlesque. There had been
topical satires before, such as Shadwell's *The Scowrers*,
which is concerned with the seventeenth-century
equivalents of the Mohocks; there had been farces;
and there had been burlesques, like *The Rehearsal*, or
Estcourt's *Prunella* (a skit on the Italian opera), or
Cibber's *The Rival Queans*. But the species were
kept rigidly separate. It was probably the novelty
of *The Mohocks* which led to its refusal by the Drury
Lane management. It is certainly a great deal better
than the average farce of the time, and I believe the
prologue ' To be Spoken by the Publisher ' does not
exaggerate its acting merits:—

This Farce, if the kind Players had thought fit
With Action had supply'd its want of Wit.
Oh Readers! had you seen the Mohocks rage,
And frighted Watchmen tremble on the Stage;

M

Had you but seen our mighty Emperor stalk;
And heard in Cloudy honest Dicky talk,
Seen Pinkethman in strutting Prig appear,
And 'midst of Danger wisely lead the Rear.

William Penkethman, 'famous for his face', and the
diminutive Dicky Norris were two low comedians
who were the darlings of the galleries at Drury Lane.

The Wife of Bath, a rubbishy comedy on conventional lines, of which Chaucer, metamorphosed into
a Queen Anne gallant, is the hero, is unimportant.
But in *The What D'Ye Call It: A Tragi-Comi-Pastoral
Farce* Gay returned to the *genre* he had created in
The Mohocks, and with greater success. The experiment, he justly claims in the preface, is more ambitious, and more effective 'in interweaving the several
Kinds of Drama with each other, so that they cannot
be distinguish'd or separated'. There are two plays
in it, as in *The Taming of the Shrew* and other
Elizabethan plays; an outer and an inner play. The
outer play, which is in prose, is negligible; Gay was
never as certain of himself, I think, in prose as in
verse. A solitary exception is provided by the
theatrical reminiscences of Sir Roger, the elderly
country J.P. who fancies himself as a dramatic
critic :—

Why neighbours, you know, experience, experience—
I remember your Harts and your Bettertons—But to see
your Othello, neighbours—how he would rave and roar,
about a foolish flower'd handkerchief!—and then he
would groul so manfully,—and he would put out the
light, and put the light out so cleverly!

That is delicious. It has almost the ring of the
mumbled and swaggering recollections of Justice

Shallow. But the interest of the piece lies in the
heroic couplets of the inner play. It is primarily a
delightful parody of the heroic tragedy and the heroic
pastoral. But the parody itself becomes creative and
develops into a miniature comedy of sentiment of
singular attraction. The process is, indeed, the same
as in *The Shepherd's Week*, which grew out of a skit
on Ambrose Philips into a new type of pastoral.

The plot in *The What D'Ye Call It* has the deliberate *naïveté* of a burlesque, but the characterization
and the background are realistic. The course of true
love is represented by the rustic lovers Kitty and
Filbert. A certain Dorcas accuses Filbert of getting
her with child, and he is taken up before the Justices
and offered the alternatives of marrying Dorcas or
going for a soldier. He chooses the army as the
lesser evil :—

> From door to door I'd sooner whine and beg,
> Both arms shot off, and on a wooden leg,
> Than marry such a trapes—No, no, I'll not.

and there is a melancholy leave-taking between Kitty
and Filbert:—

KITTY.
[*She is drawn away on one side of the Stage by* Aunt *and*
Grandmother.

Yet one look more.

FILBERT.
[*Haul'd off on the other side by the Sergeant.*
One more e'er yet we go.

KITTY

To part is death.

FILBERT.
'Tis death to part.

KITTY.

Ah !

FILBERT.

Oh !

In the army Filbert finds his old friend Peascod, who is about to be shot as a deserter :—

1 *COUNTRYMAN.*
Come, 'tis no time to talk.

2 *COUNTRYMAN.*
Repent thine ill,
And pray in this good book.   [*Gives him a Book.*

P E A S C O D.
I will, I will.
Lend me thy handkercher—The Pilgrim's pro—
[*Reads and weeps.*
(I cannot see for tears) Pro—Progress—Oh !
The Pilgrim's Progress—eighth—edi-ti-on
Lon—don—printed—for—Ni-cho-las Bod-ding-ton
With new ad-di-tions never made before.
Oh ! 'tis so moving I can read no more. [*Drops the book.*

However, Dorcas confesses that she has wronged Filbert, a reprieve comes for Peascod, and everything ends as it should.

The sentimental interest centres in Kitty. There is real pathos in her appeal to Filbert :—

I can sow plain-work, I can darn and stitch ;
I can bear sultry days and frosty weather ;
Yes, yes, my Thomas, we will go together ;
Beyond the seas together we will go,
In camps together, as at harvest glow.
This arm shall be a bolster for thy head,
I'll fetch clean straw to make my soldier's bed ;
There, while thou sleep'st, my apron o'er thee hold,
Or with it patch thy tent against the cold.
Pigs in hard rains I've watch'd, and shall I do
That for the pigs, I would not bear for you ?

And the pathos is only more affecting because of
a suspicion of irony which keeps it fresh and sweet.
There is sentiment of another sort, a transposition
into other terms of a genuine, if milder, *saeva indig-
natio* than Swift's, in the oddest scene in the play.
The three Justices are discussing 'a point of Law',
and 'a large silver tankard' is going round.

A Ghost rises.

1 GHOST.

I'm Jeffrey Cackle.—You my death shall rue;
For I was press'd by you, by you, by you.
[Pointing to the Justices.

Another Ghost rises.

2 GHOST.

I'm Smut the farrier.—You my death shall rue;
For I was press'd by you, by you, by you.

A Woman's Ghost rises.

3 GHOST.

I'm Bess that hang'd myself for Smut so true;
So owe my death to you, to you, to you.

A Ghost of an Embryo rises.

4 GHOST.

I was begot before my mother married,
Who whipt by you, of me poor child miscarried.

Another Woman's Ghost rises.

5 GHOST.

Its mother I, whom you whipt black and blue;
Both owe our deaths to you, to you, to you.
[All Ghosts shake their heads.

SIR ROGER.

Why do you shake your mealy heads at me?
You cannot say I did it.

BOTH JUSTICES.

No—nor we,

1 *G H O S T.*

All three.

2 *G H O S T.*

All three.

3 *G H O S T.*

All three.

4 *G H O S T.*

All three.

5 *G H O S T.*

All three.

A *SONG* sung dismally by a *GHOST.*

Ye goblins, and fairys,
With frisks and vagarys,
Ye fairys and goblins,
With hoppings and hobblings,
Come all, come all,
To Sir Roger's great hall.

All fairys and goblins,
All goblins and fairys,
With hoppings and hobblings,
With frisks and vagarys.

CHORUS.

Sing, goblins and fairys,
Sing, fairys and goblins,
With frisks and vagarys,
And hoppings and hobblings.

[*The ghosts dance round the Justices, who go off in a fright,
and the ghosts vanish.*

The fantasy of the scene, instead of obscuring as
sometimes in Swift, intensifies and guarantees the
social criticism.   But the primary intention was, of
course, to parody *Richard III* and *Macbeth.*   A little

pamphlet entitled *A Compleat Key to the last new Farce The What D'Ye Call It*, which is usually attributed to Benjamin Griffin (one of the Lincoln's Inn Fields actors) and Theobald, has pointed out most of the parodies in the piece. The victims, according to this tract, were Shakespeare, Dryden, Otway, Rowe, Addison, and Ambrose Philips, and most of them are parodied several times. Some of the suggestions are rather absurd, and Gay himself discusses one of them in a letter to Caryll, only to dismiss it contemptuously. 'His great charge is against "The Pilgrim's Progress" being read, which, he says, is directly levelled at Cato's reading Plato. To back this censure he goes on to tell you that "The Pilgrim's Progress" being mentioned to be the eighth edition makes the reflection evident, the tragedy of "Cato" being just eight times printed.'

The What D'Ye Call It was followed two years later by *Three Hours after Marriage*. *The What D'Ye Call It* had been a tragi-comi-pastoral farce; *Three Hours after Marriage* was a farcical comedy. It is, however, more of a farce than a comedy. The humour, and it is one of the few laughter-compelling pieces of the time, lies in a *crescendo* of absurdity in the incidents, hardly at all in the characterization or the dialogue. A deliberate defiance of probability is its key-note. The plot, so far as there is one, centres in Dr. Fossile, a fussy, dried-up antiquarian, and an obvious caricature of a contemporary eccentric, Dr. Woodward of Gresham College. The Doctor has taken it into his head to marry the young and frivolous Mrs. Townley. But the ceremony is no sooner concluded than his troubles begin with the repeated

and unexpected appearances in his house of two rakes
of the town, Plotwell and Underplot, who have
entered into a competition (with the secret connivance
of Mrs. Townley) to cuckold the doctor. The rivals
turn up in all sorts of disguises. Plotwell is now a
Dr. Lubomirski who has been expelled from Poland
for inventing a medicine which is an infallible test
of virginity, and now a mummy in the Doctor's
collection; Underplot is at one moment a patient
gasping at death's door, and at the next a stuffed and
newly acquired crocodile. But Fossile is too much
for them, and the *dénouement*, which brings Mrs.
Townley an earlier husband from the East Indies,
and rids the Doctor both of his wife and her admirers,
is only poetical justice. There is, in addition to
Fossile and his tormentors, an underplot, more satirical
than farcical, which circles round Miss Phoebe Clinket,
his extremely literary niece, who has written a tragedy
on the subject of Deucalion and Pyrrha, and whose
one, and always frustrated, ambition is to get it acted.

There are some very comic scenes in both parts of
the play. But the ludicrousness of the main plot lies
in the situations, and they can only be appreciated to
the full in their context. In one place, for instance,
a *tête à tête* between Plotwell and Mrs. Townley is
interrupted by the sound of Fossile's return. Plotwell
does not know where to hide himself, but Mrs. Townley
reassures him : —

> Arm thy self with Flounces, and fortify thy self with
> Whalebone; enter beneath the Cupolo of this Petticoat.

And Plotwell actually creeps under the immense
hooped skirt which was then fashionable, and Fossile
is outwitted. In isolation the episode is flat and more
than a little improper; in its context one notices

nothing but the comicality of the subterfuge. It is
easier to quote from the scenes in which Phoebe
Clinket is concerned. They are better written and
nearer comedy, and the emphasis is all the time on
the dialogue more than on the situation. Phoebe is
introduced in the first act, 'her maid bearing a Writing-
Desk on her Back. Clinket Writing, her Head-dress
stain'd with Ink, and Pens stuck in her Hair.' She is
called on by Plotwell, who is to father her tragedy
because the managers of the theatre 'have had the
Assurance to deny almost all my Performances the
Privelege of being Acted', and they are joined by
Sir Tremendous, 'the greatest Critick of our Age'—
a hit at Dennis—and two actors who have come to
hear the new tragedy. The reading begins with
a parody both of Dennis and of those battles of wit
which are characteristic of Wycherley's and other
Restoration comedies:—

> *Clink.* I perceive here will be a Wit-Combat between
> these Beaux-Esprits. Prue, be sure you set down all the
> Similes.   Prue *retires to the back part of the*
> *Stage with Pen and Ink.*
>
> Sir *Trem.* The Subjects of most modern Plays are as
> ill-chosen as—
> *Plotw.* The Patrons of their Dedications.
>   Clink. *makes signs to* Prue.
>
> Sir *Trem.* Their Plots are as shallow—
> *Plotw.* As those of bad Poets against new Plays.
> Sir *Trem.* Their Episodes are as little of a Peice to
> the main Action, as—
> *Clink.* A black Gown with a Pink-colour'd Petticoat.
> Mark that Prue.   [*aside.*
> Sir *Trem.* Their Sentiments are so very delicate—
> *Plotw.* That like whipt Syllabub they are lost before
> they are tasted.

At last Clinket begins to read the tragedy : —

> *Clink.* The first Speech has all the Fire of Lee.
> > *Tho' Heav'n wrings all the Sponges of the Sky,*
> > *And pours down Clouds, at once each Cloud a Sea,*
> > *Not the Spring-Tides—*
> *Sir Trem.* There were no Spring-Tides in the Mediterranean, and consequently Deucalion could not make the Simile.
> *Clink.* A Man of Deucalion's Quality might have travelled beyond the Mediterranean, and so your Objection is answered. Observe, Sir Tremendous, the Tenderness of Otway, in the Answer of Pyrrha.
> > *Why do the Stays*
> > *Taper my Waste, but for thy circling Arms?*
> *Sir Trem.* Ah! Anachronisms! Stays are a modern Habit, and the whole Scene is monstrous, and against the Rules of Tragedy.

When the actors also join in condemning the play Clinket (who has been pretending all the time that it is Plotwell's) is so overcome with fury that she goes off in a faint from which she only recovers when Fossile starts throwing her manuscripts into the fire—'The tag of the Acts of a new Comedy! a Prologue sent by a Person of Quality! three copies of recommendatory Verses! and two Greek Mottoes!'

Three Hours after Marriage was produced and published in Gay's name, but in a prefatory 'Advertisement' he admitted 'the Assistance I have receiv'd in this Piece from two of my Friends; who, tho' they will not allow me the Honour of having their Names join'd with mine, cannot deprive me of the Pleasure of making this Acknowledgement'. The two anonymous collaborators were Pope and Arbuthnot. Pope seems to have been responsible for Clinket, and Gay for the scenes with Fossile, Townley, Plotwell, and Underplot. Arbuthnot probably helped with Fossile—Woodward was one of his particular *bêtes noires*—and may also be assumed to have contributed the medical and scientific jargon with which the play is filled. To-day the farce is remembered primarily as a literary curiosity, and the world of scholarship is still busily identifying the individuals satirized in it. Was Phoebe Clinket meant to be the Countess of Winchelsea or Mrs. Centlivre? Was Mrs. Townley a caricature of Mrs. Mead? Was Plotwell a dig at Cibber? Was the Countess of Hippokekoana intended for the Duchess of Monmouth? The questions are not without their interest and importance, since the personalities of the play provoked a whole host of pamphlets in abuse of the three poets, which in their turn were ultimately responsible for *The Dunciad*. But they have been too often allowed to overshadow the merits of the piece, topical satire or not, simply as a play.

An interval of eleven years separates the production of *Three Hours after Marriage* from the first performance of *The Beggar's Opera*, but it includes nothing more significant than *The Captives*, a not uninteresting tragedy which ran for a week at Drury Lane in 1724, and the pleasant, but unacted, pastoral of *Dione*. In the interval Gay had made and lost a fortune in the South Sea Bubble, and had come to fancy himself slighted by the Court and feared by Walpole. It will not be necessary to expatiate upon the *furore The Beggar's Opera* created in 1728. The story has been told over and over again, but perhaps most effectively in the note to the variorum *Dunciad* of 1729. The vast success of it was unprecedented, and almost

incredible : What is related of the wonderful effects
of the ancient Music or Tragedy hardly came up to it :
Sophocles and Euripides were less follow'd and famous.
It was acted in London sixty-three days, uninterrupted;
and renew'd the next season with equal applause.   It
spread into all the great towns of England, was play'd
in many places to the 30th, and 40th time, at Bath and
Bristol 50, &c.   It made its progress into Wales, Scotland,
and Ireland, where it was performed 24 days together.
The fame of it was not confin'd to the author only ; the
Ladies carry'd about with 'em the favourite songs of it
in Fans ; and houses were furnish'd with it in Screens.
The person who acted Polly, till then obscure, became all
at once the favourite of the town ; her Pictures were in-
graved and sold in great numbers ; her Life was written ;
books of Letters and Verses to her publish'd, and pamphlets made even of her Sayings and Jests.

The Beggar's Opera carried one stage farther the
experiments of *The Mohocks, The What D'Ye Call It*,
and *Three Hours after Marriage*.   It represented
a fusion of at least five distinct *genres* : it was a topical
satire ; it was a farce; it was a comedy of sentiment;
and it was a burlesque, not only of the heroic tragedy,
then on its last legs, but of the infinitely more popular
and influential Italian opera.   The topical elements
do not require to be emphasized.   'Robin of Bagshot,
alias Gorgon, alias Bluff Bob, alias Carbuncle, alias
Bob Booty ', who 'spends his life among women',
was an obvious caricature of Walpole, and the
Peachum-Lockit quarrel and Macheath's embarrassing
position between Polly and Lucy—'How happy
could I be with either '—were not less obvious
reflections of Walpole's breach with Townshend, and
of the difficulties he sometimes found himself in
between Lady Walpole and Molly Skerrett.   There

are other topical references. Peachum, for example, is evidently modelled upon that thorough-paced scoundrel, 'the Moriarty of the Eighteenth Century, Jonathan Wild; and Mrs. Peachum may perhaps have been the Duchess of Kendal.[1]

The farcical elements in the piece are less prominent and less important. But once or twice a phrase comes up that, with its unexpected absurdity, is the very quintessence of farce. Such is Peachum's rebuke to Polly :—

Married ? the Captain is a bold man, and will risque any thing for money ; to be sure he believes her a fortune. Do you think that your mother and I should have liv'd comfortably so long together, if ever we had been married ? Baggage !

And one or two of the episodes, e. g. the ready recovery of Mrs. Peachum's temper under the influence of 'cordial', are frankly, almost crudely, farcical.

The problem of 'sentiment' is more difficult. It is disconcerting to have to label Macheath a sentimental character ; he is altogether too much of the reckless libertine, too much of the dashing soldier of fortune. But one has only to compare him with the conventional rakes of Restoration comedy, the Horners and the Celadons, to realize that his place is even less with them. I believe that Macheath, like Tom Jones, belongs to the school of a kind of secondary sentimentalism ; one may call it the school of good inten-

[1] The identification is new. It was suggested by a sentence in Spiller's dedication of the second edition of Bullock's *Woman's Revenge* to 'Pretty Miss Polly Peachum' :—
Mr. John Gay . . . has Metamorphosed Mr. John Marston's Dutch Curtezan, into the Duchess of — and your Mother Acts the Part, and does not prove her Marriage.

tions.   The sentimentalism of Cibber and Steele lay
in an emotional conception of conventional morality.
The sentimentalism of Gay, as earlier of Farquhar
and later of Fielding, lay in the not less emotional
conception that a good heart will cover a multitude
of sins.   It is less explicit in Gay than in the others
because of the prevailing irony; but it may be read
between the lines.   Macheath is a little too jovial
and generous and good-natured to be a convincing
highwayman.   'What a fool is a fond wench!' he
soliloquizes, 'Polly is most confoundedly bit—I love
the sex.   And a man who loves money, might as well
be contented with one guinea, as I with one woman.'
But we will not believe him; he is deceiving himself,
but he cannot deceive us.   We know that his heart
is with Polly, and when he brings the play to an end
with 'Ladies, I hope you will give me leave to
present a Partner to each of you.   And (if I may
without offence) for this time, I take Polly for mine.—
And for life, you Slut,—for we were really marry'd.—
As for the rest.—But at present keep your own
secret', we know that he knows it too.   Polly is
more obviously a sentimental character.   She is a
romantic little person with a conception of love quite
inappropriate in one of her station.   'I did not marry
him,' she tells the horrified Mr. and Mrs. Peachum,
'(as 'tis the fashion) cooly and deliberately for honour
or money.   But, I love him.'   And she reposes an
infinite confidence in the novels and plays Macheath
lends her.   Mrs. Peachum was probably quite right
in suspecting that 'Those cussed Play-books she reads
have been her ruin'; and even Macheath has to play
up to the role of knight-errant for which he is cast
in her imagination.

Polly. And are *you* as fond as ever, my dear?

Mach. Suspect my honour, my courage, suspect any thing but my love—May my pistols miss fire, and my mare slip her shoulder while I am pursu'd, if ever I forsake thee!

Polly. Nay, my dear, I have no reason to doubt you, for I find in the Romance you lent me, none of the great Heroes were ever false in love.

There is more than a little of Biddy Tipkin in Polly Peachum.

The burlesque does not, as in *The What D'Ye Call It*, take the form of a direct parody.[1] It is rather a generalized satire upon the ridiculous features common to all the tragedies and operas of the time. Lucy's nicely melodramatic attempt to poison Polly is a case in point. The final *peripeteia*, which saves Macheath from the gallows (and which some thick-headed critics called surrendering the 'moral for a joke, like a fine gentleman in conversation') is another; and the satire, in this case, is pointed by the beggar's confession— 'you must allow, that in this kind of Drama, 'tis no matter how absurdly things are brought about.'

The Beggar's Opera was the climax of Gay's career as a dramatist; it was not, however, his last work. In the four years that intervened between its production and his death he found time to write four more plays and to recast at least one, and perhaps two, of his earlier pieces. *The Distress'd Wife*, a satirical-sentimental comedy of the Cibber type produced and published posthumously, and *The Rehearsal at Goatham*, a pleasant anti-Walpole farce, are com-

[1] Though Swift was told that the Peachum-Lockit quarrel was intended to parody the quarrel between Brutus and Cassius in *Julius Caesar.*

paratively trivial.   Swift, with all his partiality for
Gay, was compelled to admit to Pope that *The Distress'd Wife* was 'a very poor performance'.   The two
ballad-operas, *Polly* and *Achilles*, are more important.

Polly was the sequel which the success of *The
Beggar's Opera* had made inevitable.   An 'Introduction' between the 'Poet' and a 'Player'—analogous
to the scene with the beggar which begins *The Beggar's
Opera*—explains sufficiently candidly its *raison d'être*,
'the inducement of gain'.   *Polly* was written, primarily, to make money.   In this respect it was even
more successful than *The Beggar's Opera*—it brought
Gay some £3,000—but the success was wholly a
success of scandal.   Walpole, still smarting under the
lashes of *The Beggar's Opera*, refused to permit its production; it is possible he may have fancied that he was
lampooned in Ducat; and the action provided an
advertisement which gave the play a factitious popularity in print that it would never have won, on its
own merits, on the stage.

Polly, certainly, was not worth £3,000; but it is
a better play than it is customary to admit: inferior,
no doubt, to *The Beggar's Opera* or Sheridan's *Duenna*,
but infinitely superior to the average ballad opera of
the eighteenth century.   It is in the songs, in particular, that the inferiority is most evident.   They are
careless and clumsy, quite without the epigrammatic
quality of the songs in *The Beggar's Opera*.   But the
dialogue is not markedly inferior, and the characterization, though Polly and Macheath are almost un-
recognizable, is more than adequate.   The plot is
more of a melodrama than a burlesque.   Macheath
has been transported to the West Indies, and has
escaped from captivity, and turned pirate.   In order,

however, to evade the attentions of his numerous wives he has been compelled to black his face and assume the name of Morano. Polly, still faithful to his memory, has crossed ' the herring-pond'[1] to join him, but her money is stolen and she has to enter into the service of the amorous Ducat. She escapes from him by dressing up as a man, and falls in with the pirates, but does not recognize Macheath, and is not recognized by him. There are adventures and misadventures with the pirates and their enemies the Indians, and when the curtain goes down Macheath is dead and Polly is about to marry Cawwawkee the Indian prince.

It is all more than a little suggestive of *Peter Pan*, a fantastic farce, a light-hearted melodrama; and as such it has both charms and excitements. But the full effect is spoilt by a decided sententiousness. The sneers at the courtiers and the politicians were a little wearisome even in *The Beggar's Opera*. In *Polly*, what with Cawwawkee the 'noble savage' and his not less noble father Poketokee (the Tories), and the pirates and Mr. Ducat (the Whigs), they are a perfect nuisance. Gay's social conscience had never been very robust. 'Gay was remarkable', Pope told Spence, 'for an unwillingness to offend the great, by any of his writings'. It is, indeed, obvious. But there was sincerity, if it did not go very far, in the satire of *The What D'Ye Call It* of 1715. It was different in 1729. Gay had become fat and middle-aged; he had lost his ideals and his illusions, and their place had been taken by personal spite and a cheap cynicism borrowed, without being understood, from Swift and

---

[1] One of the earliest uses of the phrase. The *N.E.D.* only records two earlier, in 1686 and 1689.

Pope. This is why this song of Jenny's, though it is better written than most, rings so false :—

> Honour plays a bubble's part,
>   Ever bilk'd and cheated;
> Never in ambition's heart,
>   Int'rest there is seated.
> Honour was in use of yore,
>   Tho' by want attended :
> Since 'twas talk'd of, and no more;
>   Lord, how times are mended!

It is a kind of inverted hypocrisy, Mr. Pecksniff in Timon's shoes.

Achilles, Gay's swan-song—it was acted two months after his death—is a more satisfying piece than *Polly* ; ' of his very best manner, a true original ', Pope wrote to Caryll. Usually described as a burlesque of the classical myth of Achilles's concealment at Scyros in a woman's dress, it is more properly a modernization of the same kind as Mr. Shaw's *Caesar and Cleopatra*. Gay has adopted the old myth and the legendary figures—Achilles, Thetis, Ajax, Ulysses, and the others—but he has treated them as if they had been his own contemporaries of the eighteenth century. Mr. Shaw has done the same, and Shakespeare had done it before either of them. The effect is belittling, of course, but it is not belittling in the way a bur- lesque is.

The humour, naturally, is principally the humour of the unexpected. It is most effective, because it is most unexpected, in the first scene of the play. ' Have you then no Regard to my Presentiment ? ' Thetis asks Achilles; ' I can't bear the Thoughts of your going, for I know that odious Siege of Troy wou'd be the

Death of thee.' And there is much more in this vein.
Perhaps the most amusing stroke is Achilles's reference
to the centaur Chiron—'I dare swear that good
Creature is now so distress'd for the Loss of me, that
he will quite founder himself with galloping from
Place to Place to look after me.' But humour of this
sort is not the only attractive feature in *Achilles*.
The dialogue is admirably bright and pointed, and
there is a refreshing diminution of the 'hits' and the
'strokes' at the Court and the Government, the
lawyers and the doctors. The songs, too, are well
turned. Consider these lines:—

> Such Homage to her Beauty,
>   What Coyness can reject?
> Accept, as 'tis your Duty,
>   The Tribute with Respect.
> What more can Beauty gain thee?
>   With Love 1 offer Power.
> What Shame can ever stain thee,
>   Restrain thee,
>   Or pain thee,
> When blest with such a Dower?

It is not poetry, perhaps, but it is the perfection of
verse-making.

iii

Gay has been the victim recently of some unintelli-
gent pedantry and much uninstructed enthusiasm. It
is to be hoped that Dr. Dryasdust and Mr. Puff will
soon have done their worst. The elaborate disinter-
ment we have seen, not only on the stage but in
erudite treatises and luxuriously limited editions, of
The Beggar's Opera and *Polly*, is not likely to be

repeated. But Gay's vogue has not been entirely fruitless, even from the point of view of critical appreciation. Mr. Oswald Doughty's introduction to his edition of *Polly* was sensible and unpretentious; Mr. G. C. Faber produced an almost impeccable edition of the *Poetical Works*—including most of the plays; and Mr. Osbert Burdett discussed the operas in his *Critical Essays* with an admirable acuteness.

Mr. Burdett's analysis of the literary qualities of the songs in *The Beggar's Opera* was particularly opportune. The music, of course, counts for much; but it does not explain the unique buoyancy and fascination of the songs. They are, in fact, as good poetry as music. One has only to listen to the lilting cadences in Macheath's songs:

> If the heart of a man is deprest with cares,
> The mist is dispell'd when a woman appears;
> Like the notes of a fiddle, she sweetly, sweetly
> Raises the spirits, and charms our ears.

'Like the notes of a fiddle, she sweetly, sweetly '—it is as exquisitely melodic as anything in Campion or Dr. Bridges. Gay has often been compared, as a librettist, with Gilbert; but the collocation is preposterous. Gilbert's verse is 'slick', with the deadly facility of facetiousness. It is never, except perhaps once or twice in *The 'Bab' Ballads*, poetry. But Gay's happiest songs are pure poetry—'pure poetry' almost, in Mr. George Moore's sense; bright and coloured, like the images they introduce, never earthy, never ponderous.

Our Polly is a sad slut! nor heeds what we have taught her.
I wonder any man alive will ever rear a daughter!

For she must have both hoods and gowns, and hoops to
  swell her pride,
With scarfs and stays, and gloves and lace; and she will
  have men beside;
And when she's drest with care and cost, all-tempting,
  fine and gay,
As men should serve a Cowcumber, she flings herself away.

Only a poet of the nicest verbal tact would have
dared to introduce the 'Cowcumber'. But how vividly
right it is!

Mr. Burdett was more challenging when he
attempted to set Gay beside Swift and Congreve as
one of the masters of English prose. 'If an anthology
were compiled', he claimed, 'of Strict Prose, in the
interest of that neglected art, Gay would have an
important place in it. He would have to be set aside
Swift and Congreve. A comparison of his dialogue
with that of Congreve would reveal the fineness of
Gay's ear. No one's dialogue is more idiomatic and
more beautiful.' They were brave words, but I think
injudicious. The charged vehemence of Swift's prose,
the haunting disillusioned cadences of Congreve's,
were beyond Gay. The prose of *The Beggar's Opera*
and *Polly* and *Achilles* (the earlier prose may be neglected) is good certainly, but its distinguishing characteristic is a determined unemotionality. It is prose
that is primarily the perfectly adequate mechanism
of expression. It is easy, because it is unambitious;
it is lucid, because it never means more than it says;
there are no undertones or overtones. Gay's prose is
nearer Peacock's than any other English writer; it
is a long way from Swift and Congreve.

Dr. Johnson was disappointed not to find in Gay
'in any great degree the *mens divinior*, the dignity of

genius'. We need not share his disappointment. The *mens divinior* in the eighteenth century tended to be another name either for the pompous classical tragedy, like Johnson's own *Irene*, or the lumbering sublimities of the Pindaric ode. It is, of course, obvious that Gay was not of the first rank. 'Charm' rather than the *mens divinior* was his most notable possession, and 'charm' is not so much a positive quality as that *aurea mediocritas* which is the effect of the *absence* of any outstanding positive qualities. His versatility was a reflection of the fact that he could not do anything supremely well; his 'balance' meant that he did not take anything very seriously. It is not, however, necessary to be always supreme or sublime. There is a place, in literature as in life, for irony, and Gay is one of the few masters of irony in English. He has a peculiar irony of his own, as distinct from the teasing irony of Pope as from the indignant irony of Swift. Suaver, more assured, it is characterized by a stereoscopic ability to assume at one time two or more points of view. It is possible to see in *The What D'Ye Call It* at once a pastoral and a parody of the pastoral, and in *The Beggar's Opera* a genuine as well as a burlesque opera. The Kitty of *The What D'Ye Call It* is not only an exposure of, but also a plea for the simple life; and the Polly of *The Beggar's Opera* is equally a real character of sentiment and a caricature of sentimentalism. An irony of this kind could only be the product of a mind intellectually and imaginatively agile. I believe that Gay's intelligence was freer than that of any of his contemporaries, except Congreve. Addison, Swift, Pope, and Defoe, though they saw farther, did not see as clearly as Gay. They were the victims of certain prepossessions—emotional, political, and moral—which the shallower Gay escaped. That is why he seems so much more ' modern ' than the others. In Swift and Pope, and still more in Addison and Defoe, the reader is always coming up against the limitations which the eighteenth century imposed. It is the principal justification of the genial scepticism which did duty for a philosophy with Gay that it was blandly innocent and unconscious of these limitations.

VI

HENRY CAREY

i

HENRY CAREY, 'hymning Harry Carey', is believed to have been an illegitimate son of George Savile, the famous Marquis of Halifax. As a boy he was a member of Addison's little senate at Button's, but music, and not literature, eventually became his profession. He was, however, 'but slenderly accomplish'd in his art', and 'his chief employment was teaching at boarding-schools, and among people of middling rank in private families'. He committed suicide at his house in Great Warner Street, Clerkenwell, in October 1743.

Of Carey's songs and poems, only 'The Ballad of Sally in our Alley' can be said to be familiar, though 'Namby-Pamby: or, A Panegyric on the New Versification' is still occasionally referred to. A quaint medley of Ambrose Philips, nonsense and nursery rhymes, 'Namby-Pamby' is a not unamusing parody of Philips's poems to the Pulteney and Carteret children :—

> Namby-Pamby Pilly-piss,
> Rhimy pim'd on Missy-Miss ;
> Tartaretta Tartaree,
> From the Navel to the Knee ;
> That her Father's Gracy-Grace
> Might give him a Placy-place.
> He no longer writes of Mammy
> Andromache, and her Lammy,

> Hanging panging, at the Breast
> Of a Matron most distrest.
> Now the venal Poet sings
> Baby Clouts, and Baby Things;
> Baby Dolls, and Baby Houses,
> Little Misses, Little Spouses,
> Little Play-Things, little Toys,
> Little Girls, and little Boys.

But there are better things in the three editions (1713, 1720, 1729) of *Poems on several Occasions* and the later *Musical Century*, than 'Namby-Pamby'. There is the 'Bacchanalian Rant. In the Bombast Strain' which has been given the currency of *The Oxford Book of English Verse*:—

> Bacchus must now his Pow'r resign,
> I am the only God of Wine:
> It is not fit the Wretch should be
> In Competition set with me,
> Who can drink ten times more than he.

There is the 'Second Mad Song' with its pretty aftertaste of Herrick:—

> With Goblins and Fairies,
> I'll dance the Canaries,
> And Demons all round in a Ring;
> With Witches I'll fly
> Beneath the cold Sky
> And with the Screech-Owl will I sing.

And, finally, there is the charmingly improper idyll of 'Sally Sweetbread':—

> Now the good Man's from home,
> I cou'd cast away Care,
> And with some brisk Fellow
> Steal out to the Fair.

But some are too bashfull,
And others too bold,
    And Woman's Intentions
Are not to be told.

    But could I once meet,
With a spark to my Mind;
    One fit to be trusted,
I then might prove kind;
    With him I'd steal out,
And I'd range the Fair round;
    Both eating and drinking,
The best could be found.

    Oh! there I shall see
The fine Gentlemen Rakes,
    And hear the sweet Cry,
Of Beer, Ale, Wine and Cakes:
    While I in blue Apron,
And clean Linnen Gown,
    Allure all the Sparks,
From the Flirts of the Town.

Carey is the *petit bourgeois* of the Augustans; a Gay
in drugget, the Prior of the prentices. The simple
sentiment and the homely phrasing of 'Sally in our
Alley' and 'Sally Sweetbread' are as 'middle-class'
as *Robinson Crusoe* or *Pamela*. They convey the same
suggestion of a cosy fireside piety, where true love sub-
sists happily on the Bible and Poor Robin's Almanack
and the annual excursion to Bartholomew Fair. But
there is a difference, none the less. Defoe and Richardson are *bourgeois* from the inside; they have known
no other world, they will abide by no other values.
Their *bourgeoisie* is natural and instinctive; Carey's
is not. There is a faint but unmistakable flavour of
irony in his poems which betrays the condescending

interest of an outsider. It is as if St. James's were masquerading by the banks of the Fleet River. The 'Argument' which precedes 'Sally in our Alley' in the 1729 edition of *Poems on several Occasions* is significant in this connexion:

A Vulgar Error having long prevailed among many Persons, who imagine Sally Salisbury the Subject of this Ballad, the Author begs leave to undeceive and assure them, it has not the least allusion to her, he being a stranger to her very Name at the time this Song was composed. For as Innocence and Virtue were ever the Boundaries of his Muse, so in this little Poem he had no other view than to set forth the Beauty of a chaste and disinterested Passion, even in the lowest Class of human life. The real Occasion was this: A Shoemaker's 'Prentice making Holiday with his Sweet-heart, treated her with a sight of Bedlam, the Puppet-shews, the Flying-chairs, and all the Elegancies of Moor-fields: From whence proceeding to the Farthing Pipe-house, he gave her a Collation of Buns, Cheesecakes, Gammon of Bacon, Stuffed-beef, and Bottled-ale; through all which Scenes the Author dodged them (charm'd with the Simplicity of their Courtship), from whence he drew this little Sketch of Nature; but being then young and obscure he was very much ridicul'd by some of his Acquaintance for this Performance; which nevertheless made its way into the polite World, and amply recompenced him by the Applause of the divine Addison, who was pleased (more than once) to mention it with Approbation.

The truth is that Carey, like his monitor Addison, was always a spectator in the life of contemporary London. The circumstances of his profession may have confined him to 'people of middling rank', but his heart was at Button's.

ii

It is because of the burlesques of *Chrononhotontho-logos*, that 'most Tragical Tragedy, that ever was Tragediz'd by any Company of Tragedians', and *The Dragon of Wantley* that Carey has a place here. I fancy the eight other pieces—farces, operas, ballad-operas, and what-nots—for which he was responsible 'scarce would pray for resurrection'. Perhaps there is something to be said for *Nancy: or, The Parting Lovers*, a kind of idyll of the press-gang which is based, like 'Sally in our Alley', upon an incident observed by Carey himself. 'At the Beginning of the late Impress', we are told, 'the Author saw a young Fellow hurried away by a Press-Gang, and follow'd by his Sweet-heart; a very pretty Wench, and perfectly neat, tho' plain in her Dress; her Tears, her Distress, and moving Softness, drew Attention and Compassion from all who beheld her'. But in the play the senti-mental issues are obscured by the patriotic, and True-Blue, the press-gang's victim, brings the curtain down with a surprisingly martial enthusiasm :—

> Death, or Victory, now must determinate
> All Disputes with haughty Spain :
> That proud Race we'll entirely exterminate,
> Or be Masters of the Main.

Nancy was acted in December 1739, shortly after the outbreak of the Spanish war which is associated with Captain Jenkins's ear.

Chrononhotonthologos belongs to the same *genre*, that of the burlesque tragedy, as *The Rehearsal*, *Tom Thumb* (of which it is certainly a direct imitation), and *The Critic*; it is, that is to say, a parody. Never-theless, and in spite of the prologue, which makes fun of the 'big bellowing Bombast' and the 'Fiddle-Faddle Numbers',

Serenely dull, Elaborately low

of Augustan tragedy, the parody is probably the least important element in it. With Buckingham, with Fielding, and with Sheridan the caricature came first, and their success was conditioned by its immediate reference to specific passages in the particular scenes of particular plays. The delicious absurdity of such an incident as Prince Volscius's soliloquy upon his boots was primarily an exaggeration of similar, only slightly less absurd incidents in the tragedies which were being ridiculed. With Carey, on the other hand, the parody, because it is less specific, is comparatively pointless, while the absurdities of episode and verbiage, because not tied down to particular plays, soar into an empyrean of happy nonsensicality. *Chrononhotontho-logos* is, in fact, not a burlesque, but a minor classic of our 'nonsense' literature. It may derive from *The Rehearsal*, but its real place is with *The 'Bab' Ballads* or *The Jumblies*.

The play begins with Rigdum-Funnidos and Aldi-borontiphoscophornio, two courtiers of King Chro-nonhotonthologos of Queerumania, whom they are discussing. Rigdum-Funnidos is prosaically of the opinion that His Majesty is asleep; Aldiboronti-phoscophornico, who luxuriates in 'heroic' diction, is not so sure :

'tis not definitively Sleep ;
Rather a kind of Doze, a waking Slumber,
That sheds a Stupefaction o'er his Senses ;
For now he nods and snores ; anon he starts ;
Then nods and snores again ! If this be Sleep,
Tell me, ye Gods ! what mortal Man 's awake !

They are interrupted by the entry of Chrononhotonthologos, who is mumbling invectives against sleep
to himself:

> Sport not with Chrononhotonthologos,
> Thou idle Slumb'rer, thou detested Somnus :
> For if thou dost, by all the waking Pow'rs,
> I'll tear thine Eye-Balls from their Leaden-Sockets,
> And force thee to out-stare Eternity.   [*Exit in a Huff.*

The second scene, the best in the play, introduces
Queen Fadladinida and Tatlanthe :

> *Queen.* Day's Curtain's drawn, the Morn begins to
> rise,
> And waking Nature rubs her sleepy Eyes :
> The pretty little fleecy bleating Flocks,
> In Baa's harmonious warble thro' the Rocks :
> Night gathers up her Shades in sable Shrouds,
> And whispering Osiers tattle to the Clouds.
> What think you, Ladies, if an Hour we kill,
> At Basset, Ombre, Picquet, or Quadrille ?
> *Tat.*   Your Majesty was pleas'd to order Tea,
> *Queen.* My Mind is alter'd ; bring some Ratafia.
> [*They are serv'd round with a Drum.*

In the meantime the Antipodeans have invaded
Queerumania and have been defeated by Chrononhotonthologos and General Bombardinian. The Anti-
podean king is made a prisoner and Fadladinida falls
in love with him, apparently because he is 'topsy-
turvy' and 'carries his Head where his Heels should
be':

> Oh! my Tatlanthe! have you seen his Face,
> His Air, his Shape, his Mien, his ev'ry Grace,
> In what a charming Attitude he stands,
> How prettily he foots it with his Hands !
> Well, to his Arms, no to his Legs I fly,
> For I must have him, if I live or die.

At the same time Chrononhotonthologos quarrels with Bombardinian. He had been invited to the general's tent and was dissatisfied with his supper:

> *Cook.* O, pray your Majesty, spare my Life; there's some nice cold Pork in the Pantry: I'll hash it for your Majesty in a Minute.
> *Chro.* Be thou first hash'd in Hell, audacious Slave.
> [*Kills him and turns to* Bombardinian.
> Hash'd Pork! shall Chrononhotonthologos
> Be fed with Swine's Flesh, and at Second-hand?
> Now, by the Gods, thou dost insult us, General!

In the heat of the moment Bombardinian kills him. He is immediately overwhelmed with remorse:

> Ha! What have I done?
> Go, call a Coach, and let a Coach be call'd;
> And let the Man that calls it be the Caller;
> And, in his Calling, let him nothing call,
> But Coach! Coach! Coach! Oh! for a Coach, ye Gods!

and he goes out raving to return a few minutes later and stab the doctor and himself. The Queen, Aldiborontiphoscophornio and Rigdum-Funnidos are just too late.

> *Aldi.* O horrid! horrible, and horrid'st Horror!
> Our king! our General! our Cook! our Doctor!
> All dead! Stone Dead! irrecoverably dead!
> O—h! — [*All Groan, a Tragedy Groan.*

Chrononhotonthologos is not, perhaps, a triumph of nonsense. It never quite attains to the imaginative recklessness of Foote's Panjandrum, and it is without the sublimated illogicality of the seventeenth-century poet's

> If all the world were paper,
> And all the sea were ink.

It is, however, a pleasing and a praiseworthy attempt.
The nomenclature alone is, I should imagine, unique.
Chrononhotonthologos, Bombardinian, Aldiborontiphoscophornio! Marlowe's Techelles, Usumcasane,
and Peridamas dwindle into insignificance by their
side.

The Dragon of Wantley is nominally a 'Burlesque
Opera' which has been 'Alter'd from the Original
Italian of Signor Carini'. But in point of fact it is no
more a burlesque of the contemporary opera than
Chrononhotonthologos was of the contemporary tragedy.
It is just 'nonsense'. The plot is based upon the old
ballad, itself a parody of ballad extravagances. The
scene is in the Yorkshire village of Wantley, and the
curtain goes up on the triumphant progress of the local
dragon across the stage. The consternation is universal :—

> Poor Children three,
> Devoured he,
> That could not with him grapple;
> And at one Sup,
> He eat them up,
> As one would eat an Apple.

and a chorus of Nymphs and Swains join in :—

> Houses and Churches,
> To him are Geese and Turkies.

The latest exploit of the dragon has been the invasion
of the squire at his breakfast:

> He drank up all their Coffee at a Sup,
> And next devour'd their Toast and Butter up.

It is agreed that the famous Moore must be applied to,
and Margery is made the spokesman.

> Gentle Knight! all Knights exceeding,
> Pink of Prowess and good Breeding,

she begins; and concludes,

> Thus I kiss thy valiant Garment,
> Humbly hoping there's no Harm in't.

The knight succumbs to her charms and volunteers to take on the dragon. When the battle is imminent Margery becomes alarmed for her hero:—

> Sure my Stays will burst with sobbing,
> And my Heart quite crack with throbbing.
> My poor Eyes are red as Ferrets,
> And I hav'nt a Grain of Spirits.

However, her despondency is dispelled by the attack of the jealous Mauxalinda, a rejected mistress of Moore's,

> Were you as fine as e're wore Silk or Sattin,
> I'd beat your Harlot's Brains out with my Patten . . .
> D'ye laugh, you Minx! I'll make you change your Note,
> Or drive your grinning Grinders down your Throat.

> Duetto.
> Insulting Gipsey,
> You're surely tipsey,
> Or non se ipse
> To chatter so.

and then Mauxalinda gets to business:—

> Come, Bodkin, come! take Mauxalinda's Part,
> And stab her hated Rival to the Heart.

But in the nick of time ' Enter Moore, and takes away the Bodkin ', and they are reconciled. The actual battle is rather an anticlimax. Moore having got into the dragon's well we have the stage direction ' Enter Dragon, and goes to the Well ':—

Dragon. What nasty Dog has got into the Well,
   Disturbs my Drink and makes the Water
   smell.
      [Moore *pops up his Head, and cries* Boh!

Air. *Dragon.* Oh, ho! Mr. Moore,
   You Son of a Whore,
   I wish I'd known your Tricks before.
    [Moore *gets out of the Well, encounters the Dragon,*
     and kills him by a Kick on the Back-side.

The Dragon of Wantley was very much more
successful on the stage than *Chrononhotonthologos.* The
music of John Frederick Lampe may have had something to do with it. It is also true, I think, that the
humour of *The Dragon,* broader and vulgarer though
it is, is more immediately effective than the rather
rarefied nonsense of *Chrononhotonthologos.* The rough-
and-tumble of Wantley is about as easy as winking,
but it must have required an exceptionally sensitive
and intelligent audience in the eighteenth century to
relish the aimless absurdities and the finely flavoured
imbecility of Queerumania.

VII

HENRY FIELDING

i

'IT has often been a matter of wonder', Arthur Murphy wrote in the first biography of Fielding, 'that he, who most undoubtedly possessed a vein of true and genuine humour, should not have proved more successful in his theatrical productions.' It is still a matter of wonder to-day. Why is Fielding one of the greatest of novelists and too often one of the most indifferent of dramatists? How is it that the most dramatic of our romancers is the least romantic of our dramatists? The solution which Murphy propounded was that the plays were written too quickly. 'When he had contracted', he says, 'to bring on a play, or a farce, it is well known, by many of his friends now living, that he would go home rather late from a tavern, and would, the next morning, deliver a scene to the players, written upon the papers which had wrapped the tobacco, in which he so much delighted.' It is obvious that a masterpiece is not likely to be brought to birth under these conditions. Unfortunately, however, for Murphy's theory the dreariest of Fielding's plays are not those like *Pasquin*, of which he claimed to have written 'nine Scenes with Spirit in one Day', but those like *The Modern Husband* and *The Universal Gallant*, which were undoubtedly written with some care and deliberation. *Pasquin* is a very lively performance; *The Modern Husband* must be one of the dullest productions ever

fathered by a man of genius. Moreover, as Scott
pointed out long ago in his refreshingly sane essay on
Fielding, the novels were written quite as rapidly and
under precisely the same conditions as the plays. If
these haphazard methods did not interfere with the
composition of *Tom Jones*, it seems unnecessary to
assume that they were responsible for the deficiencies
of the dramas. Scott's own solution of the problem
was, however, hardly happier than Murphy's. 'The
drama', he observed, 'speaks to the eye and ear ; and
when it ceases to address these bodily organs, and
would exact from a theatrical audience that exercise
of the imagination which is necessary to follow forth
and embody circumstances neither spoken nor exhibited, there is an immediate failure, though it may be
the failure of a man of genius.' In other words,
a good novelist can never be a good dramatist. It
must be admitted that Scott seems to have put forward
the suggestion with considerable hesitation. It is
certainly sufficiently futile. What is there to be said
for a theory which leaves out of account the poetic
drama of the Greeks and the Elizabethans, which
passes by the peculiar characteristics of Fielding's
novels and plays, and which blandly overlooks the
novelists, like Le Sage and Marivaux—and since
Scott's time Hugo, Bjornson, Tchehov, Galsworthy—
who have also been successful dramatists ?

Fielding himself said that he left off writing plays
when he should have begun. That, it seems to me,
is a more plausible explanation of their comparative
inferiority. He was only twenty when his first play,
Love in several Masques, was produced ; he was thirty
when his last important play, *The Historical Register*,
first appeared at the Haymarket. Inevitably the

dramas are less mature and less profound than the novels. It goes without saying.

Fielding's dramatic productions fall into three groups, which are different in kind and in interest. There are the farces, which are uniformly slight; there are the comedies; and there are the burlesques. There is not much to be said for the comedies. 'As a dramatist', Austin Dobson decided with unusual finality, 'he has no eminence; and though his plays do not deserve the sweeping condemnation with which Macaulay once spoke of them in the House of Commons, they are not likely to attract any critics but those for whom the inferior efforts of a great genius possess a morbid fascination'. The judgement, applied to Fielding's dramatic work as a whole, is an absurd overstatement; applied to the comedies alone it is not far from the truth. They have the air of being written to a formula; they seem almost to be exercises in the manner of Wycherley and Congreve, a mere pastiche. Fielding was too original to be successfully imitative, though the realization did not come until much later. There is a passage in *Tom Jones* in which he has been thought to be criticizing himself as a dramatist. 'Vanbrugh and Congreve', it runs, 'copied nature; but they who copy them draw as unlike the present age as Hogarth would do if he was to paint a rout or a drum in the dresses of Titian and of Vandyke. In short, imitation here will not do the business. The picture must be after Nature herself.' As a generalization the argument is certainly fallacious. In their origin many admirable comedies, e. g. Shadwell's and Sheridan's, have been imitative. It is as an analysis of Fielding's own failure as a dramatist that the remarks possess interest. There are natures in which the process of imitation, which can be an inspiration, becomes an impediment. They are probably rare, but Fielding's was certainly one of them. Imitation would not do his business.

In the comedies his model, according to Murphy, was Congreve. The evidences of imitation, now in structure, now in characterization, now in phrasing, are indeed patent. *Love in several Masques* is an immature *The Way of the World; The Temple Beau* is an inferior *Love for Love; The Modern Husband* and *The Universal Gallant* are both *The Double-Dealer manqué.* Perhaps it was the glamour of Congreve's reputation which seduced him; perhaps it was the glitter of style. The attraction, at any rate, can only have been superficial; Fielding did not and could not understand Congreve. Their interests and ambitions were divergent and to some extent contradictory. Congreve's *terrain* was the small and sophisticated world of social relationships which was the common property of the Restoration dramatists. Fielding's, as he came to discover later, was that larger and simpler territory upon which Chesterfield detected the mark of the beast and which had earlier provided in its city merchants and country squires the bogeys of the comedy of manners. Congreve's interest was confined to the analysis of the gestures, eccentricities, and affectations he recorded, and he was indifferent to their mechanism and the motives behind them. His method, that is to say, was not psychological or ethical. Instinctively, it may be divined, he was constructing out of the world of social relationships, in the observation of which he spent his life, another world, an ideal cosmos, where the disillusionment of this life would be able to find a refuge. It need hardly be said that Fielding's point of view was very different. Not an analyst, though an admirable observer, not disillusioned, if sometimes exasperated, and with all his instincts ethical—the opposition could scarcely have been more complete.

Fielding's comedies might perhaps have been saved if he had been a stylist. It is 'style' in the larger sense which has preserved the comedies and farces of Dryden. As it happens the stylistic deficiencies of the novels are even more marked in the plays. It is an illuminating exercise in contrasts to set the numerous passages in Fielding by the side of the passages from Congreve from which they have been borrowed. This, for example, is Fielding's Charlotte in *The Wedding-Day* :—

> Chains !—sure being in Love is something like being in the Galleys ; and a Lover, like other Slaves, is the Subject of no other Passion but Pity : Nay, they are even more contemptible—they are meer Insects. One gives Being to Thousands with a Smile, and takes it away again with a Frown.

And this is Millamant :—

> Beauty the Lover's Gift—Lord, what is a Lover, that it can give ? Why one makes Lovers as fast as one pleases, and they live as long as one pleases, and they die as soon as one pleases : And then if one pleases one makes more.

Here, again, is Fielding's Young Boncour in *The Fathers* :—

> Why, tell me, Charles, dost thou think it not his duty who hath begot us with all those appetites and passions, to supply them to the utmost of his power ?

And this is Valentine :—

> *Val.* My Cloaths are soon put off :—But you must also divest me of Reason, Thought, Passions, Inclina-

tions, Affections, Appetites, Senses, and the huge
Train of Attendants that you begot along with me.

Sir *Samp.* Body o' me, what a many-headed Monster
have I propagated!

Val. I am of my self, a plain easie simple Creature;
and to be kept at small Expence; but the Retinue that
you gave me are craving and invincible; they are so
many Devils that you have rais'd, and will have Employment.

The words of Mercury are harsh after the songs of
Apollo.

The comedies are least unsuccessful where they are
furthest from Congreve. Thus Lord Formal, in *Love
in several Masques*, is a gross plagiarism from Vanbrugh's Lord Foppington; but he has been plagiarized
with spirit. On the subject of reading he is almost as
amusing as his original. 'Reading', he maintains, 'is
the worst Thing in the World for the Eyes; I once
gave into it, and had in a very few Months gone
through about a dozen Pages in *Cassandra*. But I
found it vastly impaired the lustre of my Eyes. I had,
Sir, in that short Time perfectly lost the direct Ogle.'
It must be admitted that Lord Formal is an exceptional figure in Fielding's comedies.

It is on similar grounds that I should except two
plays, *Don Quixote in England* and *Rape upon Rape*,
which stand very much by themselves. They are
bustling, rough-and-tumble, and recall the Elizabethans rather than the Restoration. Without pro-
fundity and without distinction, they yet depict the
surface of contemporary life with fidelity and with
vigour. *Don Quixote* is full of the flavour of the
country-side, and with Sancho, Squire Badger, and
Guzzle we are in the world, for the only time in the
plays, of *Joseph Andrews* and *Tom Jones*. In *Rape*

upon Rape the scene is laid in London, and the types of the town (Politick the amateur politician, the jovial Ramble, Sotmore the philosophic boozer) and the atmosphere of the coffee-houses, the J.P.'s court, the round house and the taverns are captured convincingly. It is a kind of foretaste of *Amelia*. Of course the two plays are not to be compared with the burlesques, but they are very much better than the other comedies.

ii

It is with the burlesques of *The Author's Farce*, *Tom Thumb*, *Pasquin*, *The Historical Register*, and possibly *Eurydice*, that Fielding must stand or fall as a dramatist. In these plays he may be said to have created a *genre* for himself, the *genre* which he has called 'Dramatick Satire'. The original suggestion, it is true, must have come from *The Rehearsal* of Buckingham and Butler; but *The Rehearsal* was primarily a burlesque, that is to say a literary parody, whereas Fielding's pieces are primarily satirical extravaganzas. They are more ambitious; they are more fantastic; they are more serious. *The Rehearsal*, with all its wit, was still *pretence* satire, a make-believe exposure, like those exploited later by Gilbert and Sullivan. *The Historical Register*, because it was not mere play, is comparable to the satires of Rabelais and Aristophanes.

The 'Dramatick Satire', in Fielding's hands, was a fluid form; but we have, in the opening scene of *The Historical Register*, a precise statement of what he considered the possibilities of the *genre*. In the first place, it was 'not of a Nature confin'd to any Rules', but on the contrary was 'avowedly irregular'. In the second place, its 'main Design' was to 'divert the Town, and bring full houses'. In the third place, its ethical justification was to consist in its success in ridiculing 'the vicious and foolish Customs of the Age, and that in a fair manner, without Fear, Favour, or ill-nature, and without Scurrility, ill Manners, or common Place'. 'I hope', says Medley (who represents Fielding), 'to expose the reigning Follies in such a manner, that Men shall laugh themselves out of them before they feel that they are touch'd'. The formula is an adaptation of the old *ridendo corrigere mores* which all the comic dramatists had paraded on their title-pages from the time of Ben Jonson. But with the Restoration dramatists, with the exception of Wycherley, the profession meant little or nothing. At the most it might involve the running to earth of a fop or an unlicked country squire. The satire evaporated into raillery. Fielding is exceptional because he took the classical formula seriously. The sequel is well known. Sir Robert Walpole was alarmed ; a licensing act was rushed through Parliament; and 'Dramatick Satire' was without its teeth.

The Author's Farce has the sub-title *The Pleasures of the Town*, and the two titles represent what are practically two distinct plays. *The Author's Farce* itself is the more interesting, partly because it is possibly autobiographical, and partly because of its pictures of Grub Street under George II; but *The Pleasures of the Town* is decidedly the more original. In the first act of the play we find the impoverished author wrangling with his landlady :—

    Mrs. *Moneywood*. Never tell me, Mr. Luckless, of your Play, and your play.—I say, I must be paid. I would no more depend on a Benefit-Night of an un-acted Play, than I wou'd on a Benefit-Ticket in an un-drawn Lottery.—Cou'd I have guess'd that I had a Poet in my House! Cou'd I have look'd for a Poet under Lac'd Cloaths!

Luck. Why not, since you may often find Poverty under them?

A moment or two later Mrs. Moneywood leaves the room:

Luck. Jack!

Jack. Sir.

Luck. Fetch my Hat hither.

Jack. It's here, Sir.

Luck. Carry it to the Pawn-broker's. And, in your way home, call at the Cook's-Shop—make Haste. So one way or other I find, my Head must always provide for my Belly.

The act concludes with Luckless quarrelling with his publisher, Mr. Bookweight, and having his tragedy rejected by two actor managers, Sparkish and Marplay, who are patently Wilks and Cibber.[1]

In the second act we proceed to Mr. Bookweight's literary factory in Grub Street and are introduced to Dash, the 'Clerk of the Ghosts and Murders', to Blotpage, the poet (with his Parnassus in Bysshe's rhyming dictionary), and to Quibble, the 'Clerk of the Libels'.

Book. Fie upon it Gentlemen! what, not at your Pens? Do you consider Mr. Quibble, that it is above a Fortnight since your Letter from a Friend in the Country was publish'd.—Is it not high time for an Answer to come out—at this rate, before your Answer is Printed your Letter will be forgot.

[1] In 1734 Fielding produced a revised version of *The Author's Farce* in which this scene was omitted (apparently because Wilks was then dead) and its place taken by some scenes between Marplay Senior and Marplay Junior ridiculing Colley and Theophilus Cibber.

Dash's murder is inquired into and a ghost is ordered
—'let this be a bloody one'; Blotpage is also ex-
amined:—

> Mr. Blotpage, what have your Lucubrations pro-
> duc'd?—[*reads.*] Poetical Advice to a certain—from
> a certain — on a certain — from a certain — Very
> good! I will say, Mr. Blotpage writes as good a Dash as
> any Man in Europe.

They are joined at this point by Index, the motto
expert, who presents his bill—

> for adapting the Motto of *Risum teneatis Amici* to a
> dozen Pamphlets—at Six Pence per each—Six Shillings.
> For *Omnia vincit amor & nos cedamus Amori*—Six Pence.
> For *Difficile est Satyram non scribere*—Six Pence . . . a Sum
> Total, for Thirty Six Latin Mottos, Eighteen Shillings;
> ditto English Seven, One Shilling and Nine Pence; ditto
> Greek Four, One Shilling.

It appears that the Greek mottos are cheaper than
the Latin because 'as no body now understands
Greek, so I may use any Sentence in that Language,
to whatsoever purpose I please'.

The third act ends up with a fantastic *anagnorisis*,
by which it is discovered that the starving Harry
Luckless is really Henry I, King of Bantam, and that his
sweetheart Harriot (the daughter of old Mrs. Moneywood) is the lost Princess Henrietta of Old Brentford.
The bulk, however, of the act is occupied by Luckless's puppet-show *The Pleasures of the Town*. The
show, as the title suggests, is a satirical survey of the
amusements of London in 1729. The scene is 'laid
on the other side of the River Styx', and it is as
spectres that the various entertainments and diversions
of Georgian London are represented. The *dramatis
personae* range from Punch to Don Tragedio (perhaps

Thomson), Sir Farcical Comick (Cibber), Dr. Orator (Henley), Signior Opera (perhaps Handel), Mounsieur Pantomime (Rich), and Mrs. Novell (perhaps Eliza Haywood). They present themselves one by one before the presiding deity, who is the Goddess of Nonsense, and attempt in their various ways to win her heart. Dr. Orator delivers a characteristically paradoxical address on fiddles:—

> The History of a Fiddle and a Fiddlestick is going to be held forth.
> A Fiddle is a Statesman: why? Because it's hollow. A Fiddlestick is a Drunkard: why? Because it loves Ros'ning.

At this point Luckless interrupts his puppet for a moment to point out its merits to the audience:—

> Gentlemen, observe how he ballances his Hands; his Left hand is the Fiddle, and his Right hand is the Fiddlestick.

And then Dr. Orator is allowed to go on:—

> A Fiddle is like a Beau's-Nose, because the Bridge is often down; a Fiddlestick is like a Mountebank, because it plays upon a Crowd.—A Fiddle is like a Stockjobber's Tongue, because it sounds different Notes; and a Fiddlestick is like a Stockjobber's Wig, because it has a great deal of Horsehair in it.[1]

---

[1] Henley was the G. K. Chesterton of the eighteenth century. Here is a specimen of his sermon *The Lord, He is God : or, The Atheist Tormented* : ' He must be a very subtle Logician, who could distinguish away the Pain of one despairing on his Death Bed, and thinking he was in Hell Fire, from real Fire : let him take his choice ; either is sufficient torture : And he must be a very refin'd Sophister, who can persuade a poor miserable Frantic, who raves on the thought that he is damn'd, and that he feels the Fire of Hell, that it is not material Fire ; where is the Use, the

Sir Farcical, on the other hand, obliges with a song :—

> Can my Goddess then forget
> Paraphonalia,
> Paraphonalia?
> Can she the Crown on another Head set,
> Than of her Paraphonalia? [1]

And the others also take a hand. But the competition is not decided when the puppet-show is brought to an abrupt end by the interruption of a Constable and Mr. Murder-text, a Presbyterian parson, who have come to arrest Luckless for abusing Nonsense— ' People of Quality are not to have their Diversions libel'd at this Rate '.

Tom Thumb, either in the original version of the first three editions or in the revised version of *The Tragedy of Tragedies*, is Fielding's most celebrated play. It is not, however, his best play. Its popularity is due partly to the fact that it kept the stage, in the debased form of Kane O'Hara's opera, until well into the nineteenth century, and partly to the accident that it inspired some of Hazlitt's most eloquent pages. But, if it is inferior to *The Historical Register* and *Pasquin*, it is not at all a bad play.

Tom Thumb, i.e. the earlier version, is a light-hearted burlesque of the heroic tragedy. The curtain goes up on two courtiers, Doodle and Noodle, who are discussing the weather.

Comfort of this Argument ? if the Torment be the same ; it is the Sensation, not the Cause, that is the Misery ; and a Fever is as grievous, whether a Heat or a Cold occasion'd it.'

[1] Cibber, in spite of his weak and squeaky voice, was vain of his singing.   The point of this particular song was the unlucky misspelling ' Paraphonalia ' for ' paraphernalia ' in the preface to *The Provok'd Husband*.

Doodle. All Nature, O my Noodle! grins for Joy.
Nood.   This Day, O Mr. Doodle! is a Day
          Indeed, a Day we never saw before.

It appears that the ' mighty Thomas Thumb ' is riding
in Triumph from the field of battle :—

Millions of Giants crowd his Chariot Wheels,
Who bite their Chains, and frown and foam like Mad-
Dogs.

The victorious general is rewarded by King Arthur
with the hand of his daughter Huncamunca. The
Queen, Dollalolla (who nurses a secret passion for
Tom) and the wicked Lord Grizzle try to prevent the
match, but they are foiled. In the interim a Bailiff
with his attendant Follower is introduced to arrest
Noodle. They find him successfully inciting Tom
Thumb to marry Huncamunca :—

Thumb. I'll hug, caress, I'll eat her up with Love.
         Whole Days, and Nights, and Years shall be
         too short
         For our Enjoyment; ev'ry Sun shall rise
         Blushing, to see us in our Bed together.
Wood. Oh, Sir! this Purpose of your Soul pursue.
Bail. Oh, Sir! I have an Action against you.
Nood. At whose Suit is it?
Bail. At your Taylor's, Sir.
        Your Taylor put this Warrant in my Hands,
        And I arrest you, Sir, at his Commands.
Thumb. Ha! Dogs! Arrest my Friend before my
         Face!
         Think you Tom Thumb will swallow this Dis-
         grace,
         But let vain Cowards threaten by their Word,
         Tom Thumb shall show his Anger by his Sword.
                          [*Kills the Bailiff.*
Bail. Oh, I am slain!

Foll. I'm murdered also,
And to the Shades, the dismal Shades below,
My Bailiff's faithful Follower I go.

The preparations for the wedding proceed until the
catastrophe intervenes. It is related by Noodle:—

I saw Tom Thumb attended by the Mob,
Twice Twenty Shoe-boys, twice two Dozen Links,
Chairmen, and Porters, Hackney-Coachmen, Whores;
When on the sudden through the Streets there came
A Cow, of larger than the usual Size,
And in a Moment, guess, oh! guess the rest,
And in a Moment, swallow'd up Tom Thumb.
King. Horrible indeed!
Ld Griz. Swallow'd she him alive?
Nood. Alive, alive, Lord Grizzle; so the Boys
Of Fishmongers do swallow gudgeons down.

And Grizzle growls to himself—

Curse on the Cow that took my Vengeance from me.

However, a 'Ghost of Tom Thumb rises'.

Ghost. Tom Thumb I am—but am not eke alive.
My Body's in the Cow, my Ghost is here.

And the disappointed Grizzle sees his opportunity:—

Thanks, O ye Stars, my Vengeance is restor'd,
Nor shalt thou fly me—for I'll kill thy Ghost.
[*Kills the Ghost.*

Swift once told Mrs. Pilkington that he had only
laughed twice in his life, 'once at some Trick a
Mountebank's Merry-Andrew play'd' and the second
time at this episode in *Tom Thumb*. It is, indeed, one
of the summits of the ridiculous.

In *The Tragedy of Tragedies*, i.e. the expanded
version of 1731, the plot was modified to introduce
Glumdalca a giantess, Foodle, a parson, and the ghost

of Gaffer Thumb. A number of verbal parodies of the heroic tragedies, together with some elaborately facetious footnotes, were also added. The additions, on the whole, are not very happy, with the exception of Lord Grizzle's famous and thrice repeated

Oh Huncamunca, Huncamunca! oh!

The footnotes, it seems to me, have been overpraised. A favourable example is provided by the line

' Millions of Giants crowd his Chariot Wheels ' :—

That learned Historian Mr. S—n [Nathaniel Salmon, 1675-1772, antiquary] in the third Number of his Criticism on our Author, takes great Pains to explode this Passage. It is, says he, difficult to guess what giants are here meant, unless the Giant Despair in the Pilgrim's Progress, or the Giant Greatness in the Royal Villain; for I have heard of no other sort of Giants in the Reign of King Arthur. Petrus Burmanus makes three Tom Thumbs, one whereof he supposes to have been the same Person whom the Greeks called Hercules, and that by these Giants are to be understood the Centaurs slain by that Heroe. Another Tom Thumb he contends to have been no other than the Hermes Trismegistus of the Antients. The third Tom Thumb he places under the Reign of King Arthur, to which third Tom Thumb, says he, the Actions of the other two were attributed. Now tho' I know that this opinion is supported by an Assertion of Justus Lipsius, *Thomam illum Thumbum non alium quam Herculem fuisse satis constat*; yet shall I venture to oppose one Line of Mr. Midwinter against them all.

In Arthur's Court, Tom Thumb did live.

But then, says Dr. B—y, if we place Tom Thumb in the Court of King Arthur, it will be proper to place that Court out of Britain, where no Giants were ever heard of. Spencer, in his Fairy Queen, is of another Opinion, where describing Albion he says.

—Far within a salvage Nation dwelt of hideous Giants.

It is mildly amusing, but it had been done before in *The Dunciad* and William Wagstaffe's *Comment upon the History of Tom Thumb*.

Pasquin is a more ambitious experiment than *Tom Thumb* or *The Author's Farce*. Like the earlier plays, it is based on *The Rehearsal*, but social and political satire of the most audacious description take the place of literary criticism as the dramatic *raison d'être*. The full title is *Pasquin. A Dramatick Satire on the Times: being the Rehearsal of Two Plays, viz.: A Comedy call'd, The Election; And a Tragedy call'd, The Life and Death of Common-Sense.* The author of the 'comedy' is Trapwit; the 'tragedy' is Fustian's; and there is a critic called Sneerwell. The comedy is a daring exposure of the bribery and corruption at a country election in the heyday of the Walpolian era. The villains of the piece are the four candidates. The Court candidates, i. e. the Whigs, are a Lord Place and a Colonel Promise; the Country, or Tory, candidates are Sir Henry Fox-chase and 'Squire Tankard. The play begins with the Mayor and Aldermen debating upon the problem of how they are to employ their votes most profitably; but they are interrupted by Lord Place and Colonel Promise before they have made up their minds.

> *Mayor.* My Lord, we are sensible of your great Power to serve this Corporation; and we do not doubt but we shall feel the Effect on't.
> *L. Place.* Gentlemen, you may depend on me; I shall do all in my Power. I shall do you some Services which are not proper at present to mention to you; in the meantime, Mr. Mayor, give me leave to squeeze you by the Hand, in assurance of my Sincerity.

At this point Trapwit, the author, intervenes.

> *Trap.* You, Mr. that Act my Lord, Bribe a little more openly if you please, or the Audience will lose that Joke, and it's one of the strongest in my whole Play.
>
> L. *Place.* Sir, I cannot possibly do it better at the Table.
>
> *Trap.* Then get all up, and come forwards to the Front of the Stage. Now, you Gentlemen that Act the Mayor and Aldermen, range your selves in a Line ; and you, my Lord, and the Colonel, come to one End, and Bribe away with Right and Left.

Lord Place and the Colonel are succeeded by Sir Harry and the 'Squire, whose bribes, though more indirect, are hardly less barefaced :—

> Mr. Alderman Stitch, your Bill is too reasonable, you certainly must lose by it : Send me in half a Dozen more Great-Coats, pray ; my Servants are the dirtiest Dogs! Mr. Damask, I believe you are afraid to trust me, by those few Yards of Silk you sent my Wife—she likes the Pattern so extremely, she is resolv'd to hang her Room with it—pray let me have a hundred Yards of it ; I shall want more of you—Mr. Timber—and you Mr. Iron, I shall get into your Books too.—

That is Sir Harry's method, and this his probably not unjustified boast :—

> Give me thy Hand, Mayor ; I hate Bribery and Corruption : if the Corporation will not suffer it self to be bribed, there shall not be a poor Man in it.

Fustian's 'tragedy', which is in blank verse of the *Tom Thumb* order, is less interesting. Firebrand (Priest of the Sun), the Lord Law, and the Lord Physick are conspiring against Queen Common-Sense.

They learn that Queen Ignorance has invaded the country,

> With a vast Power from Italy and France
> Of Singers, Fidlers, Tumblers, and Rope-dancers,

and decide to join her. Eventually Common-Sense is stabbed by Firebrand after a battle between the two armies, in which Ignorance's forces are successful. However, she reappears as a ghost and her enemies fly before her. The moral of this 'Emblematical' tragedy is given by the Queen :—

> Religion, Law and Physick was design'd
> By Heaven the greatest Blessings on Mankind ;
> But Priests, and Lawyers, and Physicians made
> These general Goods to each a private Trade ;
> With each they rob, with each they fill their Purses,
> And turn our Benefits into our Curses.

But there is more in *Pasquin* than the satire of the two plays. It is a 'Rehearsal', and some of the most amusing passages are provided by the wrangling of the two authors, the caustic comments of the critical Sneerwell, and the remarks of the actors themselves *in propriis personis*. Fielding knew the London theatres intimately, before and behind the scenes, and in his picture of the 'little things' which the managers and the dramatists had to cope with he was not exaggerating. At the very beginning it is discovered that 'the Gentleman who Plays the first Ghost is not yet up; and when he is, he has got such a Church-yard Cough, he will not be heard to the middle of the Pit'. There is no wine for the comedy and Trapwit has to send out for two pots of porter—'put it into Bottles, and it will do well enough'. A little later the actor taking Law in the Tragedy 'going without the Play-House Passage, was taken up by a Lord Chief Justice's

Warrant', and a Jew carries off one of Common-Sense's maids of honour. There are other *contretemps*, as when Common-Sense appears as a ghost before she has been killed, and it is impossible not to feel for Fustian when he unburdens himself to Sneerwell:—

Indeed a Poet undergoes a great deal before he comes to his Third Night; first with the Muses, who are humorous Ladies, and must be attended; for if they take it into their Head at any time to go abroad and leave you, you will pump your Brain in vain: Then, Sir, with the Master of a Play-house to get it acted, whom you generally follow a quarter of a Year before you know whether he will receive it or no; and then perhaps he tells you it won't do, and returns it you again, reserving the Subject, and perhaps the Name, which he brings out in his next Pantomime; but if he should receive the Play, then you must attend again to get it writ out into parts, and Rehears'd. Well, Sir, at last the Rehearsals begin; then, Sir, begins another Scene of Trouble with the Actors, some of whom don't like the Parts, and all are continually plaguing you with Alterations: At length, after having waded thro' all these Difficulties, his Play appears on the Stage, where one Man hisses out of Resentment to the Author; a Second out of Dislike to the House; a Third out of Dislike to the Actor; a Fourth out of Dislike to the Play; a Fifth for the Joke sake; a Sixth to keep all the rest in Company. Enemies abuse him, Friends give him up, the Play is damn'd, and the Author goes to the Devil, so ends the Farce.

Tumble-Down Dick: or, Phaeton in the Suds is described on the title-page as a ' Dramatick Entertainment of Walking, in Serious and Foolish Characters: Interlarded with Burlesque, Grotesque, Comick Interludes, call'd, Harlequin a Pick-Pocket. As it is Perform'd at the New Theatre in the Hay-Market.

Being ('tis hop'd) the last Entertainment that will
ever be exhibited on any Stage. Invented by the
Ingenious Monsieur Sans Esprit. The Musick com-
pos'd by the Harmonious Signior Warblerini. And
the Scenes painted by the Prodigious Mynheer Van
Bottom-Flat.' In short, it is a burlesque of the pantomime; with particular reference to the pantomimes at
Covent Garden and Lincoln's Inn Fields, with which
John Rich had been delighting the populace and
horrifying the literary world for the previous twenty
years. It is written with gusto, and some of the
scenes have that peculiar combination of satirical
audacity and absurdity which is Fielding's hall-mark.
There is a pleasant little episode in a J.P.'s parlour,
discovering 'the Justice learning to Spell of an old
School-Mistress'. 'Pray, Sir,' demands Fustian (the
same Fustian as in *Pasquin*) of Machine (the author
of the pantomime), 'who are those Characters'? 'Sir,'
Machine replies, 'That's a Justice of Peace; and the
other is a School-Mistress, teaching the Justice to
Spell; for you must know, Sir, the Justice is a very
ingenious Man, and a very great Scholar, but happen'd
to have the Misfortune in his Youth never to learn to
read.' But on the whole *Tumble-Down Dick* does
not make very entertaining reading to-day. The
satire is too personal; we cannot recapture the extraordinary animosity that Rich inspired among the
people of culture of his own day, from Pope down-
wards, and the pantomime as we know it is a very
different thing from its eighteenth-century ancestor.
The greater part of Fielding's topical satire still retains
its point, because its victims are universal and omni-
present. The corrupt politician and the inflated
orator, like the poor, are with us always. But *Tumble-*

Down Dick is the exception. It is merely topical, and it shares the fate of all *ephemera*.

Eurydice, though it was unsuccessful on its first production, is a decidedly more amusing piece. (Its failure provided Fielding with the subject of a clever *jeu d'esprit, Eurydice Hiss'd, or, A Word to the Wise*.) The play begins brilliantly with a scene on the other side of the Styx. The ghost of Mr. Spindle, a beau of the court, is welcomed by the earlier deceased Captain Weazle to the nether regions. The conversation turns to Pluto:

> Mr. *Spin.* Well; but what sort of a Fellow is the old Gentleman, the Devil, hey?
> Capt. *Weaz.* Is he? Why a very pretty sort of a Gentleman, a very fine Gentleman; but, my Dear, you have seen him five hundred times already. The Moment I saw him here, I remembered to have seen him shuffle Cards at White's and George's; to have met him often on the Exchange and in the Alley, and never missed him in or about Westminster-Hall. I will introduce you to him.
> Mr. *Spin.* Ay do. And tell him I was hanged, that will recommend me to him.
> Capt. *Weaz.* No, hanged, no; then he will take you for a poor Rogue, a sort of People he abominates so, that there are scarce any of them here. No, if you would recommend your self to him, tell him you deserved to be hanged, and was too great for the Law.

It appears that the latest sensation in Hell is the arrival of 'a very fine Singer, and his Name is Orpheus'. Mr. Spindle remembers him. 'Oh, ay! he's an Italian. Signior Orpheo—I have heard him sing in the Opera in Italy. I suppose, when he goes back again they will have him in England.' Orpheus, as in the classical myth, has come to rescue Eurydice. But unfortunately for him Eurydice is reluctant to return, though she is too much of the fine lady to say it in so many words.

> *Eur.* You may depend too surely on your Eurydice, to doubt her consent to whatever would make you happy. But—it is a long way from hence to the other World; and you know, by Experience, my Dear, I am an exceedingly bad Traveller.
>
> *Orph.* I'll carry you on my Shoulders.
>
> *Eur.* Oh dear Creature! your shoulders would fail, indeed, they would. And if I should be taken sick on the Road, what should I do? Indeed in this World, I might make a tolerable shift; but on the other side the river Styx, if I was fainting, no publick House dare sell me a Dram.

Pluto takes Orpheus's part and Proserpine stands up for Eurydice, and there is an *impasse* until it is agreed that Eurydice shall go, but that she may return if Orpheus looks back on her. The conclusion is a pleasant variation of the old story. They get as far as Charon, when Eurydice cries out, 'Help, help, I shall be drowned, I shall be drowned'. Orpheus, of course, turns round to rescue her, and she escapes jubilantly from him.

The Historical Register, For the Year 1736 is certainly Fielding's dramatic masterpiece. The satire is more trenchant, the dialogue is more incisive, the fantasy is more effective, than in the earlier plays. But the first impression is one of bewilderment. The construction is so topsy-turvy and disconnected that it is easier to consider the different episodes as unconnected entries in a non-dramatic 'Register' than as the parts of a dramatic whole. From this aspect the piece will be seen to have a unity, that of a consistent

point of view and method, of its own. The scheme
is similar to that of *Pasquin*. The play is a rehearsal,
Medley is the author, and Sowrwit and Lord Dapper
are two spectators.

The prologue is an 'Ode to the New Year' parodying
Cibber's efforts as poet laureate.

> This is a Day in Days of Yore,
> Our Fathers never saw before:
> This is a Day, 'tis one to ten,
> Our Sons will never see again.

The first scene is an ideal island which is evidently
intended to represent England, 'the Island of Corsica,
being at present the chief Scene of Politicks of all
Europe'. Five politicians are sitting round a table
discussing the foreign policy :—

> 2 *Polit.* These mighty Preparations of the Turks are
> certainly design'd against some Place or other; now,
> the Question is, What Place they are design'd against?
> And that is a Question which I cannot answer.
> 3 *Polit.* But it behoves us to be upon our Guard.
> 4 *Polit.* It does, and the Reason is, because we know
> nothing of the matter.
> 2 *Polit.* You say right, it is easy for a Man to guard
> against Dangers which he knows of, but to guard against
> Dangers which no Body knows of, requires a very great
> Politician.

They then turn to the financial situation :—

> 5 *Polit.* Hang foreign Affairs, let us apply ourselves
> to Money.
> *Omnes.* Ay, ay, ay.

At this point they are interrupted by Medley. 'Gentlemen, that over again—and be sure to snatch hastily
at the Money; you're pretty Politicians truly.' They
decide at first to tax learning, but later change it to
ignorance. 'Learning being the Property but of a

very few, and those poor ones too, I am afraid we can get little among them; whereas Ignorance will take in most of the great fortunes in the Kingdom.'

The second scene changes abruptly to 'an Auction Room, a Pulpit and Forms plac'd, and several People walking about, some seated near the Pulpit'. Mr. Hen the auctioneer (a palpable take-off of the notorious Christopher Cock) is disposing of a 'Catalogue of Curiosities which was collected by the indefatigable Pains of that celebrated Virtuoso, Peter Humdrum Esq.' It includes a 'most curious Remnant of Political Honesty' (which is knocked down for five pounds), 'a most delicate Piece of Patriotism' (for which there are no bidders), 'Three Grains of Modesty', 'One Bottle of Courage, formerly in the Possession of Lieutenant Colonel Ezekiel Pipkin, Citizen, Alderman and Tallowchandler' (which goes for five shillings), a 'very neat clear Conscience which has been worn by a judge, and a Bishop', and 'a very considerable Quantity of Interest at Court' (the bidding is brisk and goes to a thousand pounds). Finally for 'the Cardinal Virtues' eighteen pence is bid under the impression that it is a cardinal's virtues. 'I thought you had said a Cardinal's Virtues, 'Sblood Sir, I thought to have bought a Pennyworth; here's Temperance and Chastity, and a Pack of Stuff that I would not give three Farthings for?'

With equal abruptness the auction comes to an end and the two Cibbers are introduced under the names of Ground-Ivy (= Colley) and Pistol (= Theophilus). They are ridiculed sufficiently thoroughly and their places are taken by 'four Patriots from different Doors, who meet in the Center and shake Hands'. (The 'Patriots' were, in the cant of the day, the combined

Tories and discontented Whigs who made up the opposition to Walpole.) They are not treated much more handsomely than the politicians of the first scene:—

  1 *Patr.* I desire to ask you all one Question,
      Are we not a Set of miserable poor Dogs?
  Omnes. Ay, ay.
  3 *Patr.* That we are sure enough, that no body will deny.
              Enter Quidam.
  Quid. Yes, Sir, I deny it. [*All start.*] Nay, Gentlemen, let me not disturb you, I beg you will all sit down, I am come to drink a glass with you—Can Corsica be poor while there is this in it?
              [*Lays a Purse on the Table.*]

They accept Quidam's bribes and there is a dance, the inner meaning of which is explained to Sowrwit by Medley:

Sir, every one of these Patriots have a Hole in their Pockets, as Mr. Quidam the Fiddler there knows, so that he intends to make them dance till all the Money is fall'n through, which he will pick up again, and so not lose one Half-penny by his Generosity; so far from it, that he will get his Wine for nothing, and the poor People, alas! out of their own Pockets, pay the whole Reckoning. This, Sir, I think is a very pretty Pantomime Trick, and an ingenious Burlesque on all the Fourberies which the great Lun has exhibited in all his Entertainments.

With this audacious fling at Walpole (Quidam is easily recognizable) *The Historical Register* comes to an end.

iii

Fielding is the most concrete of our novelists. He had a typically eighteenth-century contempt for abstractions and abstract thinkers. (Swift's picture of the Laputan metaphysicians and Doctor Johnson's *naïf* disproof of Berkeley will be remembered.) But the trait appears in Fielding in an acute form. His intolerance was not, as it was to some extent with Swift, a matter of fashion; it was due to a certain unsuspected blind spot in himself. He had a healthy, an almost unequalled, appetite for particulars, but as a consequence he could not see very far beyond them. Except in a rudimentary way, he could not generalize. The character of Blifil in *Tom Jones* is perhaps the most striking example of his helplessness in the face of an abstract quality, but the deficiency is obvious in all his writings. As a result, the philosophy of Fielding is hardly a philosophy at all. It is a hand-to-mouth affair, including only two permanent convictions: the first a boundless confidence in ' good intentions ' (a euphemism for the instincts); the second a distrust of ' hypocrisy ' (a convenient label for what he did not understand).

Fielding's concreteness is the source of his peculiar strength. There has never been any one who has represented the surface of life so faithfully, so lovingly, so plausibly. He has only to be presented with something tangible, something definite—it may be the smiling face of the landlady of a country inn, or it may be some palpable abuse such as Walpole's bribery ; and his style immediately takes on a new vigour and alertness, the page suddenly comes to life. The peculiarity is also the explanation of his limitations. It provides the reason, for one thing, why his comedies are so much less successful than his burlesques. Restoration comedy (at least as it was practised by Wycherley, Etherege, and Congreve) was an abstract form of literature ; it moved, under the mask of a portrayal of contemporary society, in the heaven of the universals. In attempting to reproduce this form of comedy Fielding was merely groping in the dark. It was a foreign language to him; he did not understand it. Burlesque, on the other hand, came down to earth. It set up Aunt Sallies that any one, who had his eyes open and a steady hand, could not fail to knock down. Fielding rushed upon them with a whoop of delight, like Don Quixote on the windmills, and the result is that his burlesques, if the satire and irony are never very subtle, have the indisputable merits of sincerity, gusto, and vigour. They are real. The comedies are only make-believe.

The most serious blemish in Fielding's novels is their failure to achieve impersonality. The point has been well put by Leslie Stephen in what is still the most acute criticism of Fielding—the essay in *Hours in a Library*. 'Fielding will not efface himself; he is always present as chorus; he tells us what moral we ought to draw; he overflows with shrewd remarks, given in their most downright shape, instead of obliquely suggested through the medium of anecdotes; he likes to stop us as we pass through his portrait-gallery; to take us by the button-hole and expound his views of life and his criticisms of things in general. His remarks are often so admirable that we prefer the interpolations to the main current of narrative. Whether the plan is the best must depend upon the idiosyncrasy of the author; but it goes some way to explain one problem, over which Scott puzzles himself; namely, why Fielding's plays are so inferior to his novels. There are other reasons, external and internal; but it is at least clear that a man who can never retire behind his puppets is not in the dramatic frame of mind. He is always lecturing where a dramatist must be content to pull the wires. Shakespeare is really as much in his plays as Fielding in his novels; but he does not let us know it, whereas the excellent Fielding seems to be quite incapable of hiding his broad shoulders and lofty stature behind his little puppet-show.' It is obvious that the source of this peculiarity of Fielding's was again his imprisonment in the concrete. He lived in a world of particulars, and the only meaning he could extract from them was in their immediate effect upon himself. He was an egocentric, not from choice but by nature. The idiosyncracy provides an additional explanation of the inferiority of the comedies to the burlesques. Comedy is an impersonal form; it has no individual predilections or inhibitions; it is anonymous. The force behind comedy (I mean the classical comedy of a Jonson, a Congreve, or a Molière) is not this or that author, but the ideal of stability, of a norm, which is inherent in the social group to which the dramatist belongs. Burlesque, especially the peculiar type of burlesque (the 'Dramatick Satire') invented by Fielding, is also based upon an ideal of social responsibility, but its attractiveness for Fielding lay in the fact that it admitted the personal factor, his own crotchets and fancies, as well. In each of his burlesques (except *Tom Thumb*, where the footnotes take its place) there is a central character, or group of characters, that acts as a commentator upon the play as it progresses. In *The Author's Farce* it is Luckless, the 'Master of the Show'; in *Pasquin* it is the trio of Trapwit, Fustian, and Sneerwell; in *Tumble-Down Dick* it is Machine; in *The Historical Register* it is Medley. It is impossible not to see in these characters

a device which would permit Fielding to indulge in
the same comments and interpolations he was later to
employ (with less justification, it seems to me) in the
novels. They were a safety valve. In everything
but name they were *ipsissimus* Henry Fielding.

VIII

CONCLUSION

i

IT has been customary to speak of the 'decadence' of the English drama in the eighteenth century. The word is ugly, and, indeed, in the last analysis unintelligible. Is it ever possible to affix a precise meaning in literary history to a metaphor from the physical world? In a sense an empire may decay; but a literature, because it is not an organism but a collection of individual talents, can only be more or less good or bad, more or less original or imitative. The eighteenth-century critics, with more logic, preferred to speak of a 'decline'. In 1723 John Dennis, with all his faults of temper the only important literary critic between Dryden and Johnson, is to be found remarking that 'Arts and Learning have, of late, sensibly, if not precipitately, declin'd. Never did such a Crowd of ill Plays . . . appear in so short a Time.' And he adds that in the preceding ten years there had not been a single comedy that was 'worth one farthing'.

There may be disputes of words, but there can be no disputing the facts. In 1700 English comedy might have seemed to be in the dawn of a golden age. Dryden and Wycherley were still alive; Congreve, Vanbrugh, Farquhar, and Cibber had recently made their brilliant *débuts*; and Steele and Mrs. Centlivre were writing their first plays. By 1725 it had proved to have been a false dawn. Congreve and Vanbrugh had been silent for twenty years; Steele

was retiring into Wales; Farquhar and Mrs. Centlivre
were dead; and Cibber, the only survivor of the
giant race before the flood, was about to dwindle into
a poet laureate. In the places of the older writers
there were only Gay and Carey, both of them 'more
of a silver penny than a man', and a few mediocrities.
(Fielding's first play only appeared in 1728.) In
1750 the process had culminated and, with the exception of Foote, there was not a single dramatist
writing of even the third rank.

> Thy hand, great Anarch! lets the curtain fall,
> And universal Darkness buries All.

Is it possible to explain this state of affairs? Partly,
no doubt, it was just chance, the accident that between
Farquhar and Goldsmith no man or woman of specifically dramatic genius happened to be born into the
English-speaking world. But fundamentally it was
due to a change, in its turn the result of wider political
and economic changes, in the character of the theatrical
audiences. They were noticeably less select than they
had been at the Restoration. The courtiers of William
and Anne and the Georges were of a different stamp
from those of Charles and James. They were more
interested in politics than in the theatre, diplomats
rather than litterateurs, and the satellites and parasites
of the court followed in their wake. On the other
hand, a taste for the theatre had spread into the city.
Aldermen and merchants, with their apprentices and
their wives, began to come to plays more and more
regularly. They no longer found themselves ridiculed
upon the stage, at any rate less often and less brutally,
and if their morality had become less strict (a citizen
told Farquhar that 'however Pious we may appear to

be at home, yet we never go to that end of the Town
but with an intention to be Lewd ') the immorality of
the theatre was also less patent. Dennis counted
' three sorts of People now in our Audiences . . . who
were unheard of in the Reign of King Charles the
Second '. They were younger brothers ' who had
been kept at home, by reason of the pressure of the
Taxes '; profiteers ' who made their Fortunes in the
late war '; and the foreigners who were every year
coming to London in larger and · larger numbers.
Dennis's statements are confirmed by Lord William
Grimston (that ' booby Lord ' upon whose single
comedy, *The Lawyer's Fortune*, a reluctant immor-
tality has been conferred by the ridicule of Swift and
Pope and Steele), who makes his Sprightly say that
the audiences ' for the most part are ill-breed Citizens,
Jews, and Merchants' Prentices '.

One consequence of this invasion of the theatre
by the city was that comedy, the intellectual and
sophisticated plaything of the court, was being gradually supplanted, on the one side by the Italian opera,
on the other by the pantomime, the farce, and the
ballad opera. The process has been described by
Pope in the *Epistle to Augustus*:—

> What dear delight to Britons Farce affords !
> Ever the taste of Mobs, but now of Lords ;
> (Taste, that eternal wanderer, which flies
> From heads to ears, and now from ears to eyes).[1]
> The Play stands still ; damn action and discourse,
> Back fly the scenes, and enter foot and horse ;
> Pageants and Pageants, in long order drawn,
> Peers, Heralds, Bishops, Ermine, Gold and Lawn ;

[1] The allusion is explained by Warburton's note. ' From
Plays to Operas, and from Operas to Pantomimes.'

The Champion too! and, to complete the jest,
Old Edward's Armour beams on Cibber's breast.

Another consequence of the decline of the theatre in prestige was that the better writers began to avoid it. Probably the half-dozen most important literary figures between 1700 and 1750 were Swift, Pope, Defoe, Addison, Richardson, and Fielding. Of the six, Fielding, of course, was a dramatist, though he practically abandoned the theatre before he was in his thirties; but the others are only might-have-beens. Addison's single comedy, *The Drummer*, a slight thing but exceptionally charming and well put together, is sufficient evidence of what he might have done in comedy. Pope, who had a share in *Three Hours after Marriage* (a farce more often calumniated than read) would not, I fancy, have ever made a great dramatist. But what of Swift and Defoe? I like to imagine Swift's unwritten comedies—something between *Volpone* and *Troilus and Cressida*, the playthings of an exasperated idealism. As for Defoe, he might well have been a kind of Thomas Heywood, better, no doubt, but still another 'prose Shakespeare'. And then there is Richardson? But these are problems which might admit, like Sir Thomas Browne's, of a wide solution.

ii

The change in the composition of the spectators in the theatre did not, as a matter of fact, stamp out comedy altogether. It survived in an enfeebled and different form. The measure of the *difference* between the typical comedy of the Restoration and the typical comedy of the eighteenth century may be said to be the difference between 'fantasy' and 'sentiment'. But the advent of sentimentalism (which is, of course, connected with the increasingly *bourgeois* element in the audiences), though it may show why eighteenth-century comedy was different from that of the Restoration, does not explain its inferiority. There is nothing essentially false or essentially second-rate in the conception of sentimental comedy. It need only be feeble in feeble hands. The failure of eighteenth-century comedy, so far as it can be explained at all, was not primarily the fault of the dramatists but of the conditions in which they wrote. The point was made some years ago by William Archer in his extremely stimulating survey *The Old Drama and the New*, but it has not received the attention it merits.

Archer attributed the stagnation of the drama of the eighteenth century to 'material conditions'. The theatres, he believed, were too large and the lighting too dim. 'A subtler art of imitation demanded smaller theatres and better methods of lighting: and in neither of these directions did any advance take place. The drama was confined by royal letters patent to the

> houses twain
> Of Covent Garden and of Drury Lane,

with the Haymarket to fill the gap of the summer vacation. The patent houses were rebuilt several times, but always larger, not smaller. Being lit exclusively by candles, they were dim caverns in comparison even with the gas-lighted playhouses of the nineteenth century; while the exquisite regulation of lights rendered possible by electricity and other modern illuminants was entirely undreamt of. The Elizabethan platform-stage survived in the shape of a large 'apron' jutting out into the auditorium beyond the curtain line; and actors, in order to be thoroughly well heard and seen, habitually moved to the front of this apron, relinquishing all attempt to live, as it were, within the picture. Exaggeration then, whether comic or tragic, was necessarily the order of the day. The optics and acoustics of the theatre imperatively demanded it. Why should playwrights attempt a faithful reproduction of real character in its real environment, when they knew that the mechanism of the playhouse rendered such a thing impossible?'

Archer was certainly mistaken in describing the theatres of the earlier part of the century as large. They were minute. Farquhar speaks (in *A Discourse upon Comedy*) of 'five hundred saucy People' as a crowded audience; and the dimensions of Wren's Drury Lane are those of a modern tennis court. But his indictment of the lighting and the 'apron' was reasonable. And his conclusion, that exaggeration was the order of the day, was undeniably justified. He did not, however, face one fact: the fact that the successes of Wycherley, Etherege, Vanbrugh, and Congreve were obtained under precisely these 'material conditions'. If they are great dramatists, why might not their successors have been so too? Archer's fundamental mistake, in all his dramatic criticism, was that he leaned too securely on the standards of the realistic drama of his age. He was not able to realize that there have been two dramas in English: the artificial or poetic, and the naturalistic; that they do not flourish within the same 'material conditions'; and that you cannot measure Congreve by the tape of Mr. Galsworthy. The artificial comedy of Congreve and his contemporaries was born out of the crude and convention-ridden theatre of their time.

But Archer was right all the same about the eighteenth century. In its intentions the eighteenth-century drama, with some obvious exceptions, was demanding, though only half consciously, a better lighting, a better scenery, and a more suitable stage. It was, as we have seen in connexion with its sentimentalism, radically naturalistic. The tragedy is that, though it had outgrown the material conditions of the artificial drama of the seventeenth century, it was still compelled to put its new wine into those old bottles. Its history is that of the strangling of a tentative, still embryonic realism by an obsolete technique. And the apron and the candle-lighting were not the only embarrassments of the dramatist of the eighteenth century. He had to face the problems imposed by a gradually more elaborate and more expensive system of scenery. He had, that is to say, to reduce drastically the number of his scenes. And, as a consequence, he had to find something to take the place of the rapid movement which the Elizabethans had obtained by their quickly changing scenes. The modern dramatist has found this in the climax and the tableau ending. But these things are the offspring of the curtain, and the eighteenth century refused to use its curtain. (The curtain was raised after the prologue had been spoken, and was not lowered again until after the epilogue.)

The conclusion seems to be that the normal development of the comic drama of the eighteenth century, through sentimentalism to realism, was delayed and partially frustrated by the obsolete 'machinery' of the theatres. An original genius might have overridden the obstacles it imposed. But the typical dramatists of the century—the Steeles and Lillos, the Colmans and Cumberlands—with their technique borrowed from one world and their heart in another, were between the devil and the sea, and the consequence was the confusion and comparative failure of their plays. The dramatists who were most successful were not typical at all. They were either ' sports ', like Gay and Fielding, or, like Sheridan and Goldsmith, were content to return to the traditions of the previous century. The comedy of the century, so far as it was a homogeneous movement like Elizabethan and Restoration comedy, was never more than second-rate.

A BIBLIOGRAPHY
I. HISTORY AND CRITICISM

GEORGE FARQUHAR. A Discourse upon Comedy. 1702.

JOHN DENNIS. A large Account of the Taste in Poetry. 1702.

ANONYMOUS. A Comparison between the Two Stages. 1702.

GILES JACOB. The Poetical Register. 1719.

JOHN MOTTLEY. A List of all the Dramatic Authors. 1747.[1]

SAMUEL DERRICK. A General View of the Stage. 1759.[2]

DAVID ERSKINE BAKER. The Companion to the Play-House. 2 vols. 1764.

JOHN GENEST. Some Account of the English Stage. 10 vols. 1832.

A. W. WARD. A History of English Dramatic Literature. 3 vols. 1899.

G. H. NETTLETON. English Drama of the Restoration and Eighteenth Century. 1914.[3]

ERNEST BERNBAUM. The Drama of Sensibility. 1915.

G. C. D. ODELL. Shakespeare from Betterton to Irving. 2 vols. 1921.

WILLIAM ARCHER. The Old Drama and the New. 1923.

J. W. KRUTCH. Comedy and Conscience after the Restoration. 1924.

ALLARDYCE NICOLL. A History of Early Eighteenth Century Drama. 1925.

II. INDIVIDUAL AUTHORS[4]
I. COLLEY CIBBER
A. Plays

Love's Last Shift; or, The Fool in Fashion. C. 1696.

Woman's Wit; or, The Lady of Fashion. C. 1697.

Xerxes. T. 1699.

---

[1] Published with Thomas Whincop's *Scanderberg*.

[2] Published under the pseudonym 'Thomas Wilkes'.

[3] He has also an essay in *The Cambridge History of English Literature*, vol. x, ch. iv.

[4] The following abbreviations are used: C. (comedy), T. (tragedy), T.C. (tragicomedy), F. (farce), M. (masque), O. (opera), B.O. (ballad opera), Past. (pastoral), Int. (interlude), Burl. (burlesque).

The Tragical History of King Richard III. T. (1700).
Love makes a Man; or, The Fop's Fortune. C. 1701.
She wou'd, and She wou'd not; or, The Kind Impostor. C. 1703.
The Careless Husband. C. 1705.
Perolla and Izadora. T. 1706.
The School-Boy; or, The Comical Rivals. F. 1707.
The Double Gallant; or, The Sick Lady's Cure. C. (1707).
The Comical Lovers C. (1707).
The Lady's Last Stake; or, The Wife's Resentment. C. (1707).
The Rival Fools. C. (1709).
Hob, or the Country Wake. Int. 1715.
Myrtillo. M. 1715.
Venus and Adonis. M. 1716.
The Non-Juror. C. 1718.
Ximena; or, The Heroick Daughter. T. 1719.
The Refusal; or, The Ladies Philosophy. C. 1721.
Caesar in Egypt. T. 1725.
The Provok'd Husband; or, A Journey to London. C. 1728.
Love in a Riddle. B.O. 1729.
Damon and Phillida. B.O. (1729).
The Rival Queans. Burl. 1729.
Papal Tyranny in the Reign of King John. T. 1745.

B. *Collected Editions*

Plays written by Mr. Cibber. 2 vols. 1721.
The Dramatic Works of Colley Cibber. 3 vols. 1760.

C. *Biography and Criticism*

An Apology for The Life of Mr. Colley Cibber. 1740.
ANONYMOUS. The Laureat; or, The Right Side of Colley Cibber, Esq. 1740.
THOMAS DAVIES. Dramatic Miscellanies. 3 vols. 1783–84.
WILLIAM HAZLITT. Lectures on the English Comic Writers. 1818.
ISAAC DISRAELI. The Calamities and Quarrels of Authors. 1859.
DE WITT C. CROISSANT. Studies in the Work of Colley Cibber. 1912.
F. D. SENIOR. The Life and Times of Colley Cibber. 1928.

II. RICHARD STEELE

A. Plays

The Funeral: or, Grief A-la-mode. C. 1702.
The Lying Lover; or, the Ladies Friendship. C. 1704.
The Tender Husband; or, the Accomplish'd Fools. C. 1705.
The Conscious Lovers. C. 1723.
The School of Action. Fragment. 1809.
The Gentleman. Fragment. 1809.

B. Collected Editions

RICHARD STEELE. The Mermaid Series. Ed. G. A. Aitken. (1903).[1]

C. Biography and Criticism

W. M. THACKERAY. English Humourists of the Eighteenth Century. 1853.
JOHN FORSTER. Historical and Biographical Essays. 2 vols. 1858.
AUSTIN DOBSON. Richard Steele. 1888.
G. A. AITKEN. Richard Steele. 2 vols. 1889.
M. E. HARE. Steele and the Sentimental Comedy. 1909.[2]

III. SUSANNA CENTLIVRE

A. Plays

The Perjur'd Husband: or, The Adventures of Venice. T.C. 1700.
The Beau's Duel: or a Soldier for the Ladies. C. 1702.
The Stolen Heiress or the Salamanca Doctor Outplotted. C. [1703].
Love's Contrivance, or, Le Medecin malgre Lui. C. 1703.
The Gamester. C. 1705.
Love at a Venture. C. 1706.
The Basset-Table. C. 1706.
The Platonick Lady. C. 1707.
The Busie Body. C. [1709].

---

[1] There are also several eighteenth-century collections.
[2] An Essay in *Eighteenth Century Literature. An Oxford Miscellany.*

The Man's bewitch'd or, The Devil to do about Her. C. [1709].
A Bickerstaff's Burying; or, Work for the Upholders. F. [1710].
Mar-Plot; Or, The Second Part of the Busie Body. C. 1711.
The Perplex'd Lovers. C. 1712.
The Wonder: A Woman keeps a Secret. C. 1714.
The Gotham Election. F. 1715.
A Wife well Manag'd. F. 1715.
The Cruel Gift. T. 1717.
A Bold Stroke for a Wife. C. 1718.
The Artifice. C. 1723.

B. Collected Editions.

The Works of the celebrated Mrs. Centlivre. 3 vols. 1760–1761.
The Dramatic Works of the celebrated Mrs. Centlivre. 3 vols. 1872.

C. Biography and Criticism

WILLIAM HAZLITT. Lectures on the English Comic Writers. 1818.
MONA WILSON. These were Muses. 1924.

IV. JOHN GAY

A. Plays

The Mohocks. F. 1712.
The Wife of Bath. C. 1713.
The What D'Ye Call It. Burl. [1715].
Three Hours after Marriage. C. 1717.
Dione. Past. 1720.
The Captives. T. 1724.
The Beggar's Opera. B.O. 1728.
Polly. B.O. 1729.
Acis and Galatea. Past. 1732.
Achilles. B.O. 1733.
The Distress'd Wife. C. 1743.
The Rehearsal at Goatham. F. 1754.

B. Collected Editions

The Plays of John Gay. 2 vols. [1924]. [Omits The Wife of Bath and Three Hours after Marriage.]

The Poetical Works of John Gay. Ed. G. C. Faber. 1926.
[Only selections from The Wife of Bath, Three Hours after Marriage, The Distress'd Wife, The Rehearsal at Goatham.]

C. *Biography and Criticism*

SAMUEL JOHNSON. The Lives of the most eminent English Poets. 4 vols. 1781.
WILLIAM HAZLITT. Lectures on the English Poets. 1818.
LEWIS MELVILLE. Life and Letters of John Gay. 1921.
FRANK KIDSON. The Beggar's Opera. 1922.
W. E. SCHULTZ. Gay's Beggar's Opera. 1923.
OSBERT BURDETT. Critical Essays. 1925.

V. HENRY CAREY

A. *Plays*

The Contrivances; or, More Ways than One. F. 1715.
Hanging and Marriage; or, the Dead-Man's Wedding. F. [1722].
Amelia. O. 1732.
Teraminta. O. 1732.
The Tragedy of Chrononhotonthologos. Burl. 1734.
The Honest Yorkshire-Man. B.O. 1736.
The Dragon of Wantley. Burl. |1737.]
Margery: or, A Worse Plague than the Dragon. Burl. 1738.
Nancy; or, The Parting Lovers. Int. 1739.

B. *Collected Editions*

The Dramatick Works of Henry Carey. 1743.

VI. HENRY FIELDING

A. *Plays*

Love in several Masques. C. 1728.
The Temple Beau. C. 1730.
The Author's Farce; And The Pleasures of the Town. Burl. 1730.
Tom Thumb. Burl. 1730.
Rape upon Rape; or, The Justice Caught in his Own Trap. C. 1730.
The Welsh Opera: or, The Grey Mare the Better Horse. Burl. 1731.

The Letter-Writers : Or, A New Way to Keep a Wife at Home. F. 1731.
The Lottery. B.O. 1732.
The Modern Husband. C. 1732.
The Old Debauchees. F. 1732.
The Covent-Garden Tragedy. Burl. 1732.
The Mock Doctor. Or, The Dumb Lady Cur'd. B.O. 1732.
The Miser. C. 1733.
The Intriguing Chambermaid. F. 1734.
Don Quixote in England. C. 1734.
An Old Man Taught Wisdom : Or, The Virgin Unmask'd. B.O. 1735.
The Universal Gallant : or, The Different Husbands. C. 1735.
Pasquin. Burl. 1736.
Tumble-Down Dick : or, Phaeton in the Suds. Burl. 1736.
The Historical Register, For the Year 1736. Burl. [1737.|
Eurydice Hiss'd, or, A Word to the Wise. Burl. [1737.] (Published with The Historical Register).
Plutus, the God of Riches. C. 1742.
Miss Lucy in Town. B.O. 1742.
Eurydice. Burl. 1743.
The Wedding-Day. C. 1743.
The Fathers : or, The Good-Natur'd Man. C. 1778.

B. *Collected Editions*

Works, with The Life of the Author. 4 vols. 1762. Ed. Arthur Murphy. (There are later collections edited by Chalmers, J. P. Browne, Leslie Stephen, George Saintsbury, W. E. Henley, Edmund Gosse).

C. *Biography and Criticism*

ARTHUR MURPHY. An Essay on the Life and Genius of Henry Fielding, Esq. 1762 (in Works, vol. i).
WALTER SCOTT. Biographical Memoirs of Eminent Novelists. 1834.
LESLIE STEPHEN. Hours in a Library. Third Series. 1879.
AUSTIN DOBSON. Fielding. 1883.
WILBUR L. CROSS. The History of Henry Fielding. 3 vols. 1918.